THE POEM OF JOB

THE POEM OF JOB

Translated in the metre of the Original

by

EDW. G. KING, D.D.
Sidney Sussex College, Cambridge

Cambridge:
at the University Press
1914

CAMBRIDGE
UNIVERSITY PRESS

University Printing House, Cambridge CB2 8BS, United Kingdom

Published in the United States of America by Cambridge University Press, New York

Cambridge University Press is part of the University of Cambridge.

It furthers the University's mission by disseminating knowledge in the pursuit of education, learning and research at the highest international levels of excellence.

www.cambridge.org
Information on this title: www.cambridge.org/9781107685048

© Cambridge University Press 1914

First published 1914
First paperback edition 2014

A catalogue record for this publication is available from the British Library

ISBN 978-1-107-68504-8 Paperback

PREFACE

THIS little book is an attempt to translate the Book of Job
in the metre of the original according to the principle
of accented syllables which I have explained in my *Early
Religious Poetry of the Hebrews.*

It appears to me that the English language well lends
itself to this rhythm, and that much of the beauty of our
Bible Version is due to the fact that the translators, from
time to time, fall into it, all unconsciously; e.g. Job iii. 19:

> "The smáll and gréat are thére;
> And the sérvant is frée from his máster."

Here, as in the Hebrew, the rhythm depends not on the
number of syllables but on the beat of the accent.

In my translation I have consulted the Greek and Latin
versions and have freely adopted such emendations of the
text as commended themselves to my judgement, from the
Hebrew notes in Kittel's valuable *Biblia Hebraica.* In
some very few instances I have ventured to restore the text
on my own authority; but, since this book is intended for
the English reader, all reference to textual criticism has been
avoided as far as possible. I have to thank my friend the
Rev. P. J. Boyer, formerly Vicar of Rothersthorpe, for his
kindness in reading the proof-sheets.

EDW. G. KING.

GAYTON RECTORY,
   BLISWORTH.
     November 3rd, 1913.

INTRODUCTION

The unknown writer of the Book of Job must be reckoned among the greatest of the poets, whether we regard the beauty of his language or the sublime courage of his thought.

As Goethe adopted the legend of Faust so our Poet adopts the legend of Job, whose name, like that of Noah, went back to mythical antiquity (Ezek. xiv. 14, 20). This old-world name suits his purpose because he is dealing with the world-wide question of human suffering. He lays the scene of his poem, not in Israel, but in the far-off land of Uz. Since Edom was the famed home of " Wisdom " (Jer. xlix. 7 : Obad. 8), he makes Eliphaz, the Edomite, Job's oldest friend ; the other friends being also " children of the East " : for one of the aims of our Poet is to shew how feeble " Wisdom " is when confronted with the mystery of suffering: The fact that the Book of Job belongs to the " Wisdom Literature " of the Old Testament helps us to assign its date. The writer cannot be earlier than the closing years of the Captivity.

He is familiar with the Book of Deuteronomy, the late alphabetical Psalms, and the Proverbs. We must not, of course, assume that these Books would, in his time, have had the full authority of Scripture. But the popular teaching, based upon these sources, was not without danger since it maintained that righteousness would always be rewarded by prosperity. With this teaching our Poet is profoundly dissatisfied. He knows that good men, like Jeremiah, often suffer most, and that their sufferings fall upon them, not because of their sins, but because they are God's servants. He knows that Israel, as a nation, is righteous when compared with the Nations of the World; but he sees that the wicked nations prosper, while Israel not only suffers, but, in some mysterious way, suffers for God (cf. Ps. xliv. 17 ff.). He longs to find light on this old-world mystery, "Why do the righteous suffer?"

This mystery presses on him the more intensely because he has no clear view of any life beyond the grave. Nor has he any conception of what we regard as "secondary causes." In every event he sees only the direct action of God. Thus Browning makes Lúria say:

> "My own East!
> How nearer God we were! He glows above
> With scarce an intervention, presses close
> And palpitatingly, his soul o'er ours!
> We feel him, nor by painful reason know!
> The everlasting minute of creation
> Is felt there; now it is, as it was then;
> All changes at his instantaneous will,
> Not by the operation of a law
> Whose maker is elsewhere at other work."

This tells both ways. In prosperity it is sweet to feel God's hand (Job xxix. 2 ff.), but what if the despairing dreams of sickness be of His sending? (Job vii. 14: and compare Ps. viii. with Job vii. 17 ff.). How shall man know which of the "two voices" is truly the voice of God?

This problem still presses on the minds of men as in Tennyson's poem of "The two Voices," but in Old Testament times it was a far harder problem to solve; and the reader will notice that, for Job, as for Tennyson, the solution came, not to the intellect but, to the eye of faith. This, too, was through that wider view of Nature's plan which came home to Job in chaps. xxxviii.—xlii.

" So variously seem'd all things wrought,
I marvell'd how the mind was brought
To anchor by one gloomy thought;

" And wherefore rather I made choice
To commune with that barren voice,
Than him that said, 'Rejoice! rejoice!'"

Some have supposed that the Prologue (chaps. i. and ii.) and
the Epilogue (chap. xlii. 7—17), which are in prose, were actually
adopted by our Poet and incorporated in his work. This is
possible: but, if so, the episode respecting "the Satan" must
have been added by the Poet, since the conception of the Satan
dates from the Persian period (Zech. iii. 2). It is true that Satan
does not again appear after the Prologue, but the scene in
Heaven (i. 6—12: ii. 1—6), which Goethe imitates in Faust, is
needed for the Poem, since it enables the reader to see that
God may permit suffering to fall upon His servant for some good
reason beyond the ken of earth, while He regards him, all the
more, with love and sympathy. Satan departs: but Job's three
friends, Eliphaz, Bildad, and Zophar, carry on the Satan's work.
These three men are exponents of the strict orthodoxy of the
time, and, if we had fuller knowledge, we should doubtless be
able to recognise the different phases of that orthodoxy.

Eliphaz of Teman, who seems to be the eldest, claims, at
least on one occasion, to speak by inspiration (iv. 12 ff.). He is
the theologian, and his speeches contain many references to
prove from Psalms and Proverbs and other Scriptures that
prosperity and adversity are invariably assigned by God as the
reward of righteousness or as the penalty of sin[1]. He is so
convinced of this that when Job asserts his innocence he appears
to Eliphaz to be a subverter of all true religion (xv. 4, 12 f.),
and, in his third speech, he directly charges Job with grievous

---

[1] See on iv. 7—11: v. 2 f., 8—17: xv. 32 ff. &c.

sins which he *must* have committed because of his sufferings[1]. Such was the wisdom of Teman (cf. Jer. xlix. 7).

Bildad, the Shuhite, should, from the name of his clan, be akin to the Midianites (Gen. xxv. 2). He seems to represent the man of the world, and his speeches abound in homely proverbs[2] which Job treats with something very like contempt (xii. 11 f.: xxvi. 3).

Zophar, the Naamathite, is the hardest and most unfeeling of the three friends. He is the philosopher, and seems to me to represent that cold fatalism of the Wisdom literature which finds expression in such passages as Eccles. iii. 14 f. Thus, according to Zophar, the all-seeing "Wisdom" of God sees evil where men would fail to see it (xi.). God is the great inquisitor (xx.). If chapter xxvii. respecting the hidden Wisdom be also, as I believe, a portion of Zophar's last speech, then it is but a return to the thought of his first speech, that man has no power of knowing God—he cannot expect to *see* but he may well expect to *feel*—therefore his only wisdom is in obedience (xxxvii. 28).

The speeches are arranged in three cycles, though the headings are not altogether to be trusted[3].

Job replies to each of the friends in turn and, when they are silenced, he turns from man to God protesting his innocence of those sins on which the curse (in Deuteronomy) has been pronounced and challenging the Almighty to convict him (xxx., xxxi.). This challenge is answered "from the whirlwind" in the Divine speeches (xxxviii.—xlii.), which contain some of the finest poetry in the Hebrew language.

In the Divine speeches Job is not accused of *sin* but he is made to feel that God has purposes in Creation that extend to

---

[1] See xxiii. 5 ff.
[2] See viii. 11 ff. : xviii. 5—14 &c.
[3] See notes on chaps. xxvi.—xxviii.

other creatures, and other worlds, beyond the world of Man. The mystery of suffering is not hereby solved but great light is thrown upon it. When Israel began to see that God had purposes for other nations the day was not far off when suffering would be linked with expiation, and so, in becoming a *service*, would lose its sting.

But, more than this, the Divine speeches suggest to the thoughtful mind a limitation, self-imposed by God in Creation, making Him too a sharer in the struggle. Those who have studied Blake's *Illustrations of the Book of Job* will know what I mean.

Job had known before the *power* of God (ix. 1 ff., 32 f.) and so far from the thought being a help it had driven him into rebellion (vii. 17—21: ix. 22: x. 7: xiv. 16 f.: xix. 6 ff.). But now he sees that, in creation, the Divine power must submit to limitation and must work with infinite patience. It is this that moves Job to repent of his rash words. He has misjudged his best Friend.

This conception of the purposes of the Creator is nothing less than a new revelation to Job. All his former knowledge of God seemed to him to have been but *hearsay* compared with his present *sight* (xlii. 5 f.).

To our minds the Poem might have ended with these words. The Epilogue, which follows, is in prose, and we must confess that it is somewhat of the nature of an anti-climax. But perhaps there was no other way whereby the writer could bring home to his contemporaries the fact that the Suffering Servant was to receive "the double" (cf. Is. xl. 2: lxi. 7), and that God preferred an honest search for truth, even if it bordered on presumption, to the cruel orthodoxy of thoughtless minds. Thus, in the Epilogue, Job receives twice as much as he had before; and the three friends, who supposed themselves to have been defending God, are only forgiven by God upon Job's intercession.

The Elihu episode.

I have placed chaps. xxxii.—xxxvii., which contain the speech of Elihu, in an Appendix. The chapters are undoubtedly the work of a later writer who supposed that the problem of suffering could be solved by dwelling upon its remedial purpose (xxxiii. 16 ff.: xxxvi. 8 ff.), but since he has no conception of the solidarity of the race his words, though often beautiful and true, leave the problem unsolved.

Elihu probably objected (xxxii. 13) to the Divine speeches as anthropomorphic and lacking in reverence. He borrows largely from them (xxxvi. 27—xxxvii. 24) and may have intended thereby to supplant them: but there is, I think, this difference, that whereas the Divine speeches suggest a Divine *care* the same subjects when treated by Elihu suggest only a Divine *power*.

THE BOOK OF JOB

THE PROLOGUE (Chaps. I—II)

*A prose version of the story of Job, probably older than
the Poem (cf. Ezek. xiv. 14, 20), utilised by the Poet
with great artistic effect. "Mark the perfect man,
and behold the upright : for the end of that man is
peace" (Ps. xxxvii. 37). How far is this true ?*

1 1   There was a man in the land of Uz, whose name was
Job ; and that man was blameless and upright, and one
2 that feared God and that turned from evil. And there
were born unto him seven sons and three daughters.
3 His substance also was seven thousand sheep, and three
thousand camels, and five hundred yoke of oxen, and five
hundred she-asses, and a very great household ; so that
this man was greater than all the children of the East.

*His life was one perpetual round of joy and
family piety.*

4   And his sons used to go and hold feast in each one's
house in turn and would send and invite their three sisters

v. 1. Such a man, according to the teaching of the Alphabetical
Psalms, would therefore inherit every kind of earthly blessing. Compare especially Ps. xxxvii. 27, 37 ; xxxiv. 14 (15) ; cxii. 1, 2, 4. It
will be noted that these Psalms are all Alphabetical.

5 to eat and drink with them.   And it was so, when
the days of their feasting had run their cycle, that Job
used to send and sanctify them, and would rise up early
in the morning and would offer burnt offerings according
to the number of them all : for Job would say, It may
be that my sons have sinned and have renounced God
in their hearts.   Thus did Job continually.

*The scene now changes from earth to Heaven.   The
integrity of Job is there proclaimed by Jahveh but
questioned by the Satan (or Adversary).   Compare
Zech. iii.*

^a I.e. *the Angels*

6   Now the day arrived when the Sons of God^a came to
present themselves before Jahveh.   And there came also
the Adversary among them.

7   And Jahveh said to the Adversary, Whence comest
thou ?   And the Adversary answered Jahveh and said,
From going to and fro in the earth, and from walking
up and down in it.

8   And Jahveh said to the Adversary, Hast thou con-

v. 5.   Since there were seven sons the cycle would end on the
seventh day.   Thus we have a kind of sabbath.   The object of the
Writer is to shew the continuity of Job's spiritual life and his care for
his sons to avoid even the suspicion of a sin of thought.

v. 6.   The word Satan is apt to carry with it the associations of
a later theology which here would be misleading ; I have therefore
thought it best to translate it literally by *the Adversary*.   He too has
a place among the " Sons of God " and his office is to test the reality
of man's devotion to God.

v. 8.   It will be noted that God, in heaven, confirms the verdict
that earth has passed on Job in *v.* 1.

sidered My Servant Job that there is not his like in the earth ; a man blameless and upright, that feareth God and turneth from evil ?

9   Then the Adversary answered Jahveh and said,

10   Is it for nothing that Job fears God ?   Hast not Thou Thyself made a hedge about him, and about his house, and about all that he hath on every side ?   Thou hast blessed the work of his hands, and his substance teems in the land.

11   But only put forth Thine hand, and touch all that he hath, and truly he will curse Thee to Thy face.

12   And Jahveh said to the Adversary, Behold, all that he hath is in thy power; only upon himself put not forth thy hand.

And the Adversary went forth from the presence of Jahveh.

A bolt from the blue.

13   And the day arrived when his sons and his daughters were feasting and drinking wine in their eldest brother's

14 house, when a messenger came to Job and said, The oxen were plowing, and the she-asses feeding beside

15 them ; when the Sabeans came down and took them

v. 10.   The tone of this verse is very different from that of Deuteronomy.   It raises a deep question which can only be solved by a Suffering Servant.

v. 13.   The day (see *v.* 5) on which Job had sanctified them and on which therefore, as Peake well notes, the calamity that followed could not be the result of sin.

away; and the servants they slew with the sword; and I only am escaped alone to tell thee.

16   While this one was still speaking another came and said, The fire of God is fallen from heaven, and hath burned the sheep and the servants, and consumed them; and I only am escaped alone to tell thee.

17   While this one was still speaking another came and said, The Chaldeans made three bands, and made a raid on the camels and took them, and the servants they slew with the sword; and I only am escaped alone to tell thee.

18   While this one was still speaking another came and said, Thy sons and thy daughters were feasting and

19 drinking wine in their eldest brother's house: and, behold, a great wind came from over the wilderness, and it struck the four corners of the house, so it fell on the young men, and they are dead; and I only am escaped alone to tell thee.

20   Then Job arose and rent his robe, and shaved his head, and fell down upon the ground and worshipped:

21 and he said,

> From my mother's womb I came naked,
> And naked I thither return:
> Jahveh hath given and Jahveh hath taken;
> May the Name of Jahveh be blessed.

22   In all this Job sinned not, nor charged God with unfairness[a].

[a] wrong-doing

2 1   And the day arrived when the Sons of God came to present themselves before Jahveh, and the Adversary came also among them to present himself before Jahveh.

2   And Jahveh said unto the Adversary, From whence comest thou ? And the Adversary answered Jahveh and said, From going to and fro in the earth, and from

3 walking up and down in it. And Jahveh said unto the Adversary, Hast thou considered My Servant Job that there is not his like in the earth, a man blameless and upright, that feareth God and turneth from evil ? And he is still holding fast his integrity, although thou movedst Me against him, to destroy him without cause.

4   And the Adversary answered Jahveh and said,

> Skin for skin !
> But all a man hath
> Will he give for himself.

5   But now only put forth Thy hand, and touch his bone and his flesh, and truly he will curse Thee to Thy face.

6   And Jahveh answered the Adversary, Behold he is in thine hand ; only spare his life.

7   So the Adversary went forth from the presence of

v. 1. In the Babylonian religion all the lesser gods were supposed to present themselves before Marduk on one stated day in the year to receive his orders.

v. 4. Evidently a proverb. The Adversary wishes to imply that Job, at present, has only been asked to give up that which is outside his own personal life.

v. 7. This penalty which Deuteronomy assigns to an apostate Israel here falls on the Suffering Servant.

Jahveh: and he smote Job with the terrible leprosy, from the sole of his foot to the crown of his head[a].

8   And he took to himself a potsherd to scrape himself withal; and he sat among the ashes.

The one that should have been nearest tempts Job to sin. But the Suffering Servant justifies God's judgement of him against the Adversary.

9   And his wife said unto him, Art thou still holding fast thine integrity? Renounce God and die.

10   But he said unto her, As one of the senseless women speaketh so speakest thou. Shall we receive the good from God, and shall we not receive the evil? In all this Job sinned not with his lips.

" Neither found I any to comfort me."

11   And when Job's three friends heard all this evil that was come upon him, they came each from his own place; Eliphaz the Temanite, and Bildad the Shuhite, and Zophar the Naamathite: and they made an appointment together to come to bemoan him and to comfort him.

12   And when they lifted up their eyes afar off, and could not recognise him, they lifted up their voice and wept; and they rent each one his robe, and sprinkled

v. 9. The Septuagint expands this into five verses.

v. 10. The word here translated *senseless* implies that shallowness of perception that comes from ignoring God.

v. 11. They came with the best intentions but, unconsciously, they did the Adversary's work.

13 dust upon their heads towards heaven. So they sat down with him seven days and seven nights, and none spake a word unto him : for they saw that his pain was very great.

THE POEM (Chaps. III—XLII 6)

Job's Soliloquy.

3 1 After this Job opened his mouth and cursed his day ;
   2   And Job answered and said :

      With this curse compare Jer. xx. 14—18.

3 Pérish the dáy I was bórn !
   And the níght that told mán was concéived !
4 Ás for that dáy be it dárkness ;
   Let not Gód from abóve regárd it,
   Nor líght beam fórth upón it.
5 May dárkness deep-glóom defíle it ;
   May there dwéll upón it thick-clóud ;
   Black-vápours of dáy affríght it !
6 [Ás for that níght—gloom séize it !]
   Be it sévered from dáys of the yéar,
   Not to cóme in the coúnt of the mónths.
7 Ás for that níght—be it désolate ;
   No voíce of jóy come nígh it.

v. 5. Black-vapours. A doubtful word which only occurs here.
*v. 6*ª. This line should probably be omitted as a variant of *v.* 7ª.
v. 6. Be it severed. Lit. *Let it not be joined to* (cf. Gen. xlix. 6). With different vowel points the word might be translated *Let it not rejoice* as in the R.V. But this does not suit the context.
So Macbeth says :   "Let this pernicious hour
           Stand aye accursed in the calendar."

a Text
doubtful

8 May the blásters^a of dáy curse bý it,
That are fítted to roúse Levíathan.
9 Let the stárs of its twílight be dárkened:
Let it lóng for the líght, and have nóne,
Nor rejoíce in the éye-lids of Dáwn:
10 Since it shút not the doórs of my bírth,
And só hid grief from mine éyes.
11 Why wás it I díed not at bírth?
Came fórth from the wómb and expíred?
12 To what énd did knées recéive me?
And whý were there bréasts I should súck?
13 Else nów had I láin and been quíet;
Had slépt; so rést had been míne:
14 As kíngs and earth's coúnsellors dó,
Who búild for themsélves desolátions:
15 Or as prínces dó that had góld,
Such as fíll their hoúses with sílver:

Better far never to have had consciousness.

16 Or ás an abórtion that's hídden;
As bábes that néver saw líght.

*Dreary as the grave is, it is the only rest for a
sorrow like mine.*

17 Thére the wícked cease troúbling;
And thére the wéary find rést.

v. 8. May the magicians, who have power to curse, use this day to point
their curses, as though they said, May such and such a day be like the
birth-day of Job! The second line is difficult. It probably means "Those
magicians whose dire spells have power over the Dragon in the heavens."
The Babylonians supposed that eclipses were produced by the incantations
of the Seven Evil Spirits.

v. 12. Why was I acknowledged by a father? and why did a mother give
me the breast?

v. 16ª. The text adds, "I should not have been." These words do not
suit the metre and are probably a gloss.

18 All tránquil thére are the prísoners ;
   Nor héar they the táskmaster's voíce.
19 Smáll and gréat are thére ;
   And the sláve is frée from his máster.

Life being what it is, was it fair to grant it ?

20 Oh whý gives He líght to the wrétched,
   And lífe to the sóul-embíttered ;
21 Who lóng for déath, but it cómes not ;
   Though they díg for it móre than for tréasure ;
22 Who would jóy unto éxultátion,
   Would rejoíce could they fínd the gráve ?

[*The verse which follows seems to have been displaced.
    It would read more naturally after v. 20.*]

23 To the mán whose wáy is hídden,
   Whom Gód hath hédged aroúnd ?

To think that this is God's doing makes it so hard to bear!

24 For my fóod there cómes to me síghing,
   And my gróanings are poúred forth like wáter.
25 I féar but a féar—it o'ertákes me !
   And whatéver I dréad is upón me !
26 I wás not cáreless nor éaseful
   Nor résted—yet tróuble cáme.

vv. 20 ff. Compare Omar Khayyam, Quatrain 387, Whinfield's translation :
             "Since all we gain in this abode of woe
             Is sorrow's pangs to feel and grief to know,
             Happy are they that never come at all,
             And they that, having come, the soonest go ! "

FIRST CYCLE OF SPEECHES

Eliphaz's first Speech.

*Eliphaz, who now speaks, is full of piety and eloquence.   He is sure
that the experience of all good men will bear him out.   His
allusions to the Alphabetical Psalms should be carefully noted.
All that he says is eminently correct and orthodox but, like his
companions, he does the Adversary's work because he fails to
understand Job's case.*

4 1 Then Eliphaz the Temanite answered and said:

2 Wouldst thou fáint if a wórd were véntured?
   Yet whó can withhóld from spéaking?
3 Lo, thóu hast instrúcted mány,
   And hast stréngthened the hánds that were wéak.
4 Thy wórds uphéld the stúmbler,
   Thou confírmedst the féeble knées.
5 But nów it is cóme on thysélf—and thou fáintest;
   It toúches thee clóse—thou art térrified.

*This confidence in God which you have preached to others
ought to be your own support now.*

6 Ís not relígion^a thy cónfidence?
   And thy úpright wáy thy hópe?
7 Bethínk thee, what óne ever pérished—being ínnocent?
   Or whére were the úpright cut óff?
8 I have álways seen plówers of sín
   And sówers of sórrow to réap it.

^a *thy fear
(i.e. of
God)*

vv. 3–5.   All who labour for men lay themselves open to this reproach
But how cruel it is!
          "He saved others:—himself he cannot save."
v. 7.   A long line with a sting at the end.   Compare *v.* 5.
v. 8.   The thought is exactly that of the Alphabetical Psalm xxxvii. 25
          "I have been young and now am old,
          Yet never saw a righteous man forsaken."
Compare also Prov. xxii. 8 for the comparison of sowing and reaping.

9 By the bréath of Gód they pérish,
   And énd in the blást of His ánger.
10 The róaring and voíce of the líon
   And the téeth of the yóung-lions are bróken.
11 The stróng-lion may díe lacking préy
   And the whélps of the líoness be scáttered.

*In a passage of great poetical beauty Eliphaz relates how the revela-
tion of God's transcendent holiness came home to himself.*

12 Now to mé a thíng was revéaled[a],
   And mine éar caught a whísper theréof,
13 In thoúghts from the vísions of níght,
   When déep-sleep fálls on mén,
14 A féar beféll me and trémbling,
   That pút all my bónes in féar.
15 Then a spírit glíded befóre me;—
   The háir of my flésh stood eréct;—
16 It stóod,—I discérned not its fáce;
   A fórm was befóre mine éyes:
   Then a stíll (small) voíce I could héar!

     And this was the message of the voice;—

17 Can mórtal stand ríght with[b] Gód?
   Can mán be cléan with his Máker?
18 Lo, He pútteth no trúst in His sérvants[c];
   And accoúnteth His ángels impérfect:
19 What thén of dwéllers in cláy,
   Whose véry foundátion is dúst,
   Who are crúshed as quíckly as móths[d]?

[a] Or, *a thought was conveyed*

[b] Or, *in comparison with*

[c] Cf. Chap. xv. 15

[d] Cf. Ps. xxxix. 11

v. 9. Again compare Ps. xxxvii. 20.

vv. 10 f. In *v.* 10ᵃ there are two words for *lion*. The key to the passage is the Alphabetical Psalm xxxiv. 10 "Young lions may need and may hunger." See context.

vv. 19–21. Compared with God's eternity, what is human life but as the dance of the may-fly?

20 They are bróken from mórning to évening[a]:

Unregárding they pérish for éver.

21 Ís not their tént-cord remóved[a]?

They díe, and thát without wísdom!

Eliphaz now appeals to the experience of the "wise" and orthodox and quotes the thoughts of the Alphabetical Psalm xxxvii. as to the fate of evil men and the folly of envying their prosperity.

5 1 Cáll now; is there ány will ánswer?

And to whích of the sáints wilt thou túrn?

2 For impátience[b] kílleth the fóolish[b],

And jéalousy sláyeth the símpleton.

3 As for mé I have séen a fóol—taking róot,

But his cómeliness[c] sóon became rótten.

4 His sóns are fár from sáfety,

Crúshed in the gáte, unhélped,

5 Whose hárvest the húngry éateth,

(Gléaning it oút from the thórns,)

And the thírsty swállow their súbstance.

The thought of harvest suggests that what a man sows that also he reaps.

6 For nót from the dúst comes afflíction,

Nor doth sórrow spring úp from the gróund,

[a] Is. xxxviii. 12
[b] Prov. xxvii. 3; Ps. xxxvii. 1, 8
[c] Vulg.

v. 1. The word here translated *saints*, lit. *holy ones*, is often applied to the angels, but here it denotes the holy men to whose experience Eliphaz appeals.

v. 2. The reference is to such teaching as that of the Alphabetical Psalm xxxvii. 1 f., 8 f. "Fret not thyself about the evil-doers, Be not jealous about the workers of iniquity."..."Cease from anger and forsake wrath; Fret not thyself—it merely tends to harm, For evil-doers shall be cut off &c."

v. 3ᵃ. Another example of the long line of four beats.

v. 3ᵇ. *Became rotten.* I adopt the slight correction of the text suggested in Kittel's edition.

Eliphaz is again alluding to Ps. xxxvii. 35 f. "I have seen the wicked tyrannically strong, Outspreading like a verdant native tree. One but passed —and lo, he was gone &c."

7 That mán should be bórn to sórrow
  As the spárks mount úp in flíght.

*You, Job, as I hinted before (iv. 8), must have been sowing this
sorrow; therefore, if I were in your case, I would remember such
Scriptures as Ps. cvii., which tell us that when men "cry unto the
Lord in their affliction, He delivereth them out of their distress."*

8 Now Í[a] would séek unto Gód,   [a] Emphatic
  Unto Gód would entrúst my caúse;

9 Who dóeth great thíngs unséarchable[b];   [b] Ps. cxlv. 3
  Márvellous thíngs without númber;

10 Who gíveth ráin on the éarth
   And séndeth forth wáter[c] on fíelds;   [c] Ps. cvii. 35

11 So sétting the lówly on hígh[d]   [d] Ps. cvii. 41
   While moúrners are tówered in sáfety[d].

12 He frústrates[e] the plóts of the cráfty,   [e] Ps. xxxiii. 10
   So their hánds effect nóthing of wórth;

13 He táketh the wíse by their cráft[f],   [f] Ps. ix. 15
   So the coúnsel of the fróward is made rásh.

14 They encoúnter dárkness in dáy-time
   And grópe in nóontide as níght[g],   [g] Deut. xxviii. 29

15 So He sáves, from that swórd-mouth of théirs,
   The póor from the hánd of the stróng.

16 So there cómes to be hópe for the néedy,   [h] Ps. cvii. 42
   And "iníquity stóppeth her móuth[h]."

17 Lo, háppy the mán God corrécteth[i]:   [i] Ps. xciv. 12; Prov. iii. 12
   Then despíse[j] not the chástening of Shaddái,   [j] Prov. iii. 11

v. 7. A very doubtful verse. The usual translation, "But man is born to
sorrow," would seem to contradict *v.* 6.

vv. 10, 11, 16. The allusions to Ps. cvii. are rather in the thought than in
the language. When Job replies, in Chap. xii., the similarity of thought is
still closer.

v. 17. The thought is exactly that of Ps. xciv. 12 and it should be noted
that whereas, in the Psalm, the context alludes to Deut. xxxii. 36, the context
in our present passage alludes to Deut. xxxii. 39. See my Note on Ps. xciv.
in *Psalms in Three Collections*, pp. 399 f.

^a Deut.
xxxii. 39

18 For Hé, though He páins, binds úp;
    He wóunds, and His hánds make whóle^a.
19 In síx afflíctions He frées thee;
    Yea, in séven no évil can toúch thee.
20 In fámine He redéems thee from déath;
    And in wár from the pówer of the swórd.
21 From the scóurge of the tóngue thou shalt híde thee;
    Nor féar when there cómeth destrúction.
22 At destrúction and déarth thou shalt láugh;
    Neither féar thou the béasts of the éarth.
23 With the stónes of the fíeld is thy cóvenant;
    The fíeld-beasts are péaceable wíth thee.
24 Thou shalt knów thy tént to be péace;
    Shalt vísit thy fóld and miss nóthing.
25 Thou shalt knów thy séed as abúndant;
    Thy óffspring as gráss of the éarth.

^b Chap.
xxx. 2

26 Thou shalt cóme to thy gráve in ripe-áge^b;
    As the shéaf taken úp in its séason.
27 Lo thís we have seárched, so it ís;

^c See
Sept.

    Wé^c know it, do thóu mark it tóo.

vv. 19–23. The security of the righteous, hidden in God, from famine, death, war, sword, pestilence, &c. should be compared with another Psalm in this same group, viz. Ps. xci. 3–8. I have shewn elsewhere that this group of Psalms is closely related to Deut. xxxii., xxxiii.

v. 23. In Prov. xvi. 7 we read "When a man's ways please Jahveh He maketh even his enemies to be at peace with him."

Spenser's story of Una and the Lion will illustrate our verse.

"The lion would not leave her desolate,
    But with her went along, as a strong guard
    Of her chaste person, and a faithful mate
    Of her sad troubles and misfortunes hard:
    Still, when she slept, he kept both watch and ward;
    And, when she waked, he waited diligent,
    With humble service to her will prepared:
From her fair eyes he took commandé-ment,
And ever by her looks conceivéd her intent."

Job's first Reply.

6 1 And Job answered and said :

It is easy for Eliphaz to quote Ps. xxxvii. as to the folly of
"impatience" or to hint at such passages as Prov. xxvii. 3 as
to the "weight of a fool's impatience." There is something else
to be weighed, and that is the affliction that calls it forth.

2 Wóuld my "impátience" were wéighed
With my húrt in the bálance agáinst it !

3 For nów 'twould outwéigh the sea sánd :
This is whý my wórds run wíld.

4 For in mé are the árrows of Shaddái ;
My spírit drínks their póison :
God's térrors are mústered agáinst me.

And your insipid truisms ? How do they help me ?

5 Doth the wíld-ass bráy over gráss ?
Or the ox ? doth he lów over fódder ?

6 Can the tásteless be éaten unsálted ?
Or is sávour in whíte of an égg ?

7 My sóul refúses to toúch them ;
They áre as the fóod that I lóathe.

Again, you talk about my dying in a "ripe old age" (chap. v. 26).
Do I look like it ? Have I anything left to live for ?

8 Oh wóuld that I hád my reqúest,
And that Gód would gránt my desíre !

9 That Gód would pléase to crúsh me ;
To lét loose His hánd and énd me !

vv. 2, 3. It is my *hurt*, not my *impatience*, that is "heavier than the sand,"
Prov. xxvii. 3.

v. 6. Job answers proverbs with proverbs.
The words translated *white of an egg* are uncertain.

v. 7. If the text here is correct it would refer to the proverbs of which
Eliphaz was so fond.

10 Still thís consolátion were míne

ᵃ Gloss.
Text un-
certain

    [Though I ... in pain unsparing]ᵃ

    That I híd not the wórds of the Hóly One.

11 Whát is my stréngth if I wáit?

    Or mine énd that Í should be pátient?

12 My stréngth, is it stréngth as of stónes?

    Or ís my flésh as of bráss?

Job's words now become tender and pathetic. He feels that he is losing his hold on God and needs a friend's hand all the more. But his friends have proved false in his hour of need.

13 If Í have no hélp in mysélf,

    Efficiency dríven quite fróm me,

14 To the féeble a fríend should shew kíndness

    Lest the féar of Shaddái he forsáke.

15 My bréthren prove fálse as the tórrent,

    As the stréam of the tórrents that pass awáy;

16 Which are túrbid by réason of íce,

    When the snów doth híde itself ín them:

17 What tíme they wax wárm they vánish,

    When 'tis hót they are scórched from their pláce.

18 The páths of their wáy are divérted;

ᵇ *in space*

    They ascénd and pérish in vóidᵇ.

19 The caraváns of Téman looked fór them;

    The cómpanies of Shéba were hóping—

20 They were shámed becaúse of their trúst;

    They cáme there and blúshed for shámе.

v. 10. The text is corrupt. A prophet "hides" God's word if he keeps back anything of the truth (I Sam. iii. 17 f.). Job has at least the consolation of knowing that he has been honest.

vv. 15–20. This beautiful passage pictures the water-courses in the desert (cf. Ps. xlii. 1 (2); Joel i. 20), marked out as they would be, by a line of verdure promising water to the thirsting caravans—but, alas, in vain! The heat has scorched them dry. The travellers come with hope but turn away in despair. Such was Job's hope, such his experience of friendship.

Such is Job's experience and yet he only asked for sympathy.

21 So yé too becóme to me[a] nów;   [a] Sept.
Ye féel the féar and are fríghtened.

22 Did I sáy (to you), "Gíve unto mé"?
Or, "Bríbe for me oút of your súbstance"?

23 Or, "Delíver me from hánd of the énemy"?
Or, "From pówer of týrants redéem me"?

Job is willing to listen to reason.

24 Teách me, and Í will be sílent:
Shéw me whereín I have érred.

25 How swéet is hónest spéech!
But whát does your árguing árgue?

26 Do ye thínk to use sáyings for árguments?
Then the wórds of the hópeless are wínd!

27 As wéll cast (lóts) for[b] the órphan,   [b] Or, *cast*
Or make mérchandise oút of your fríend!   *yourselves*
                                                  on

Is Job's sense of right and wrong so perverted that he
cannot tell what is fair and what is not?

28 Now kíndly look mé in the fáce;
I shall súrely not líe to your fáce!

29 Retúrn, let there nót be injústice;
Retúrn, I stíll hold me ríght.

30 Ís then my táste pervérted?
Háve I no sénse of wróng?

v. 21.   I follow Kittel's text as approved by Driver.

vv. 25 f.   The words here translated *argue, arguments* may signify *reprove, reproofs.*

vv. 28 f.   I think it probable that in both these verses we have instances of a gloss or duplicate reading. If we were to omit *v.* 28[b] and *v.* 29[a] the sense would be improved.

v. 30.   We are forced to paraphrase this verse. Job here uses the words *tongue* and *palate* not of tasting food but of intellectual discernment.

*Job's own sorrow leads him to pronounce on human life as a whole.
But he returns to his own case which does but illustrate a world
of sorrow.*

7 1 Has not mán upon eárth a wárfareᵃ?
    Áre not his dáys as an híreling's?
2 As the sláve doth lóng for the évening,
    And the híreling lóoks for his wáge,
3 So I'm pórtioned to mónths of vánity,
    Níghts of tróuble appóinted me!

[*A passage in prose now follows which must be regarded
as a gloss.*]

4 If I lie down I say, "When shall I arise?" but the night
is long; and I am full of tossings to and fro until the
dawning of the day.
5 My flesh is clothed in corruption and clods of dust; my
skin closeth up and breaketh out afresh.

6 My dáys are swífter than shúttle
    And they cóme to an énd without hópe.

Job appeals to God. Compare Ps. xxxix.

7 Remémber my lífe is but wínd:
    Ne'er agáin can mine éye behold góod:

vv. 1 ff. Davidson quotes Tennyson:
    "That loss is common would not make
        My own less bitter, rather more;
        Too common! Never morning wore
    To evening, but some heart did break."
vv. 7–10. Job has no knowledge of a life beyond the grave. He may
sometimes speak of a vague existence in Sheôl. But it is not life.
It is in this spirit that Swinburne says of man:
    "In his heart is a vain desire;
        In his eyes foreknowledge of death;
    He weaves, and is clothed with derision;
        Sows, and he shall not reap;
    His life is a watch or a vision
        Between a sleep and a sleep."

8 Nor the éye see me móre that behólds me.
  Thine ówn eyes shall lóok—but I ám not.
9 Like a clóud dispélled and góne,
  He that góes to Sheól returns nót.
10 He cómes not báck to his hoúse;
   His haúnts regárd him no móre.

Job is moved by his friends' unkindness to speak bitterly of God.

11 So then Í ᵃ will no lónger refráin;
   I will spéak out my ánguish of spírit,
   Will compláin in bítterness of sóul.
12 Ám I a Séa, or a Mónster
   That Thou séttest a wátch over mé ?
13 When I sáy, "My coúch shall consóle me,
   My béd shall reliéve my compláint";
14 Thén Thou dost scáre me with dréams;
   With vísions dost máke me afráid:
15 Só that my sóul would choose strángling,
   Déath could I spúrn through my páins.
16 I wóuld not líve for éver:
   Let bé! My dáys are mere bréath ᵇ.

ᵃ Emphatic

ᵇ Ps. xxxix. 5, 11

Job now, in bitterness, reverses the thought of Psalm viii.

17 What is mán that Thóu shouldst make múch of him,
   And shouldst sét Thine héart upón him,

v. 12. *Am I a Sea....* In the Babylonian story Tiamat, "the Deep," was the Monster of unrule who had to be subdued by God. Cf. chaps. xxvi. 12; xxxviii. 8.

v. 15ᵇ. The text has *my bones*; but Kittel's text suggests a change of one letter whereby we can read *my pains*. This I accept. But the line is too short, while the next line (16ᵃ) is too long for the metre; I therefore read the verb *I could spurn* with 15ᵇ instead of with 16ᵃ, where it is quite out of place.

v. 16. The student will notice that the thought, both here and in *v.* 19, is identical with that of Ps. xxxix. 5, 11. The whole of this Psalm should be studied in connexion with the Book of Job.

v. 17. Did the cruel orthodoxy of Job's friends drive him to parody Ps. viii. 4 ?

2—2

a Ps.
lxxiii. 14;
Is. l. 4
b Ps.
xxxix. 13

c *Set me as
a mark.*
Cf. Lam.
iii. 12

d See
Sept.

18 Shouldst vísit him mórning by mórning[a],
    And tést him móment by móment?
19 Wilt Thou néver look óff[b] from mé,
    Nor léave me a swállowing-spáce?
20 If I sín what ís it I dó
    Unto Thée, Thou Wátcher of mén?
    Why didst máke me to clásh[c] with Thée,
    And to bé to mysélf a búrden?
21 Why shoúldst Thou not béar my transgréssion,
    And máke mine iníquity vánish?
    For nów I shall líe in the dúst,
    Thou mayst séek me but Í am no móre.

Bildad's first Speech.

8 1 Then answered Bildad the Shuhite, and said:

*God cannot do wrong; therefore the fault must somehow rest with
Job. Bildad is the Polonius among the friends. He is incapable
of original thought but is full of the wise sayings of the ancients.*

2 How lóng wilt thou spéak these thíngs,
    The wórds of thy móuth a stórm-blast?
3 Can Gód miscárry in júdgement?
    Can Shaddái miscárry in ríght?
4 If thy sóns have sínned agaínst Him,
    Then by méans of their sín He despátched them.
5 And[d] thóu shouldst séek unto Gód,
    To Shaddái shouldst máke supplicátion;

v. 20 f. We may compare the Quatrain (126) of Omar Khayyam:
    "Since 'twas the Master did these creatures frame,
    Why doth he cast them to disgrace and shame?
    If they are formed aright, why doth he crush them?
    And if awry, to whom belongs the blame?"
vv. 3 ff. Bildad's argument (?) may be stated thus: "God cannot do wrong.
Your sons are dead; therefore they must have deserved their fate. You are
still alive, therefore you may still have a chance to make your peace with God."

6 So if thóu^a wert púre and úpright
　He sóon would ánswer thy práyer^b
　And prósper thy ríghteous dwélling.
7 So thy fírst estáte should seem smáll,
　Thy látter end gRówing so gréat.

Bildad appeals to the "Wisdom" of the past (cf. Deut. iv. 32).

8 For ásk now the fórmer áge,
　And cón what their fáthers searched oút:
9 (For wé are of yésterday, knów-nothings,
　Our dáys upon eárth but a shádow:)
10 Will théy^c not téach thee and téll thee,
　And bríng forth wórds from their héart?

*Bildad gives specimens of this proverbial philosophy to shew
that all sorrow has sin at its root.*

11 Does the rúsh shoot úp without míre?
　Does the flág grow hígh without wáter?
12 Though stíll it be gréen and uncút
　It wíthers^d befóre any hérb.
13 So fáres it with áll God-forgétters;
　Yea, the hópe of the hýpocrite périshes:
14 His cónfidence ís as a góssamer^e
　And his trúst as a spíder's wéb^f.
15 He léans on his hoúse and it stánds not,
　He grásps, but it cánnot abíde.

*The life of man depends upon the "ground" of its "confidence," whether
the world or God. It is therefore often compared to that of a
tree, Jer. xvii. 5–8: Ps. i. and especially Ps. xxxvii. 35, 36, to
which Eliphaz has already alluded, and to which both Eliphaz
and Bildad recur in Chaps. xv. 30–33 and xviii. 16.*

16 Thóugh he be gréen in full sún
　And his bRánches o'er-shóot his gárden,

^a Emphatic
^b See Sept.

^c Emphatic

^d I.e. a-part from water

^e See Driver
^f Lit. house

17 With his róots entwíned round a spríng;
   Though he hóld him fást among stónes;
18 Yet whén from his pláce he's destróyed
   It deníes him, "I néver behéld thee."
19 Lo thís is the "jóy" of his wáy,
   And óthers spring oút from the sóil.

*Bildad closes his sermon with the pious hope that even in
Job's sad case there may be room for repentance.*

20 God néver casts óff the úpright,
   But neíther uphólds He wrong-dóers.
21 He might stíll fill thy móuth with láughter,
   And thy líps with a shóut-of-jóy:
22 Thy fóes might be clóthed with sháme,
   And the tént of the wícked exíst not.

Job's second Reply.

9 1 And Job answered and said:

*Job scornfully admits a certain truth in Bildad's last words, but
shews him that the terms " upright " and "ill-doers" cannot be
determined by a human standard but only by God's judgement
which he (Job) is seeking in vain.*

2 No doúbt!—I knów that it ís so:
   But hów is man "júst" with Gód?
3 Though with Hím he'd desíre to pléad
   He'd not ánswer him óne in a thóusand.
4 Wise-héarted! and míghty in stréngth;
   Who éver braved Hím with impúnity?

v. 19.   The thought is very similar to that of Ps. xlix. 13 to which Bildad
may unconsciously allude in *v.* 14 in the somewhat unusual word which we
translate *confidence.*

Joy.   The word is used in Is. viii. 6 "and (their) joy is in Rezin and
Eemaliah's son." But in both passages there is a bitter irony.

It is easy to speak of God's power.—But what Job seeks
is something more than omnipotence.

5 He remóveth móuntains uncónscious,
  When He thróweth them dówn in His ánger.
6 He convúlseth the eárth from her pláce,
  So her píllars go rócking to píeces.
7 He spéaks to the Sún—and it shínes^a not,
  He séals up the (líght of) the stárs,
8 He spréadeth out the héavens all alóne,
  And tréadeth the high-pláces of the séa.
9 He máketh the Béar and Oríon,
  The Pleíades and chámbers of the Sóuth.
10 He dóeth great thíngs, unséarchable;
  Yea, márvellous thíngs without númber.

But God's power is one thing, the justice of His action
is another.

11 Lo! He góeth by mé, but I sée not;
  Passes bý, but I cánnot percéive Him.
12 Lo! He spríngs^b—and whó turns Him báck?
  To Hím who shall sáy, "What wóuldst Thou?"
13 God wíll not restráin His ánger;
  Proud hélpers^c are húmbled benéath Him.

  The picture is now drawn from a law-court.

14 Much léss can Í give Him ánswer,
  Or chóose out my wórds in debáte.
15 Though ínnocent, no ánswer were míne.
  My oppónent I háve to appéase!
16 Had I cíted and Hé had respónded;
  I cóuld not trúst He would lísten.
17 Fór with a témpest He'd crúsh me,
  And múltiply woúnds without caúse,

^a Lit. *rises not*

^b I.e. *on the prey*

^c *helpers of Rahab,* i.e. Rahab and her crew

ᵃ Lam.
iii. 15

18 Not súffer me dráw my bréath,
   But would fíll me with bítter-plágues ᵃ.

19 Is it stréngth ?—(He replíes) "Here am Í."
   Is it láw ?—(then) "Whó will impléad Me ?"

20 Though ríght, His móuth would condémn me,
   Though blámeless, would próve me in wróng.

*Job takes his life in his hand and charges God with callous indifference
to all justice. The government of the world is not merely un-
moral, it is immoral.*

21 Blámeless I ám—I cáre not:
   This lífe of míne I despíse.

22 'Tis all óne; and thérefore I sáy,
   "He destróys both blámeless and wícked."

23 When the scóurge doth bríng quick-déath,
   He mócks the distréss of the ínnocent.

24 Eárth is made óver to the wícked:
   He véileth the fáce of its júdges.
   If it bé not Hé, who thén?

Job returns to his own case.

ᵇ I.e. *a
courier*

25 My dáys are swífter than a rúnner ᵇ;
   They are fléd having séen no góod.

26 They shoot bý like skíffs of réed,
   Or like éagle that swóops on the préy.

27 If I sáy, "My pláint I'll forgét,
   I'll léave (wry) fáce and be chéerful ᶜ,"

ᶜ Chap. x.
20;
Ps. xxxix.
13 (14)

28 Then of áll my páins I'm in dréad:
   I knów Thou wilt nót let me óff.

29 It is Í that háve to be gúilty,
   Why thén do I lábour in váin?

v. 20. The text reads "my mouth"; Siegfried suggests "His mouth."
This certainly suits the context, and it is easy to understand the motive for
the change.

30 Could I wásh me in wáter of snów,
   And cléanse my hánds with lýe[a],
31 Thén in the dítch Thou wouldst plúnge me,
   Só mine own clóthes would abhór me.

Job craves for a humanity in God.

32 Not a mán like mysélf I might ánswer,
   So we cáme togéther for júdgement.
33 Nor ís there a dáys-man[b] betwéen us,
   That might láy his hánd on us bóth.
34 Let Him líft His ród from óff me,
   And His térror nót overáwe me;
35 Thén would I spéak and not féar,
   For it ís not só in my cónscience.
10 1 My sóul is wéary of lífe;
   I will gíve free cóurse to my pláint;
 2 Will spéak in the bítterness of my sóul[c].
   Will sáy unto Gód, Condémn not:
   Shew me whý Thy conténtion is wíth me.
 3 Is it góod to Thée to oppréss,
   To spúrn the tóil of Thine hánds,
   And shíne on the cóunsel of the wícked?
 4 Are éyes of flésh then Thíne,
   Dost sée as frail-mán sées?
 5 Are Thy dáys as dáys of mórtals,
   Or Thy yéars as the dáys of mán,
 6 That Thóu shouldst séek out my gúilt,
   Ánd for my sín make séarch?
 7 Thou knówest me nót to be gúilty,
   And nóne can delíver from Thy hánd.

[a] Jer. ii. 22

[b] Umpire

[c] Cf. chap. vii. 11

*Job now develops the thought he had touched in verse 3ᵇ. Verses 8–12
seem to be a bitter commentary on Ps. cxxxix. 13–17. Where
shall Job find the true mind of God? Was it (as the Psalmist
argues) in the kindness of the past or (as Job fears) in the
unkindness of the present?*

8 Thy hánds toiled ón me and máde me
    Compléte;—And Thóu dost destróy me!
9 Remémber how Thou mádest me as cláy,
    And art brínging me báck unto dúst.
10 Dídst Thou not póur me as mílk
    And cúrdle me líke unto chéese,
11 Clóthe me with skín and flésh,
    And knít me with bónes and sínews?
12 Thou didst gránt me lífe and fávour,
    And Thy próvidence guárded my spírit.

^a I.e. *these
afflictions*

13 Yet thís ª Thou didst híde in Thy héart!
    I knów that thís was Thy púrpose!

14 Íf I should sín Thou dost márk me,
    And nót let me óff from my púnishment.
15 Íf I be wícked—Woe's mé!
    If ríght—I múst not lift héad.

^b ? Gloss
^c I.e. *my
head*

    [Shame-sáted and fúll of afflíction!] ᵇ
16 If it ᶜ líft Thou wilt húnt as a líon
    And agáin play the wónder upón me.

v. 9. The Potter is breaking His own vessel. Compare Omar Khayyam
    " There is a chalice made with art profound,
       And with its Maker's approbation crowned;
          Yet the world's Potter takes his masterpiece,
       And dashes it to pieces on the ground!"
vv. 14 f. In Job's present state of mind he feels that God *is* extreme to
mark what is done amiss and, as for greater sins, woe to the sinner!
    v. 16. The picture is that of a wild beast playing with its helpless victim
and striking it again if it should venture to move.

17 Thou renéwest Thy wítness agáinst me,
    And incréasest the ánger Thou béarest me.
    Reláys^a of a hóst are upón me.

a I.e.
trouble up-
on trouble

18 Then whý bring me fórth from the wómb ?
    I had díed and no éye had séen me ;
19 Had béen as thóugh I had nót been !
    Bórne from the wómb to the gráve !

Job returns to the thought he had expressed in vii. 16 f.

20 Áre not my dáys^b but féw ?
    Let Him léave me spáce to chéer up^c
21 Befóre I be góne—without retúrn—
    To the lánd of dárkness and déath-shade,
22 A lánd of gloóm-thick dárk,
    Of déath-shade withoút any órder,
    Where the shíne itsélf is as gloóm !

b Ps.
xxxix. 5f.
c Ps.
xxxix. 13
(14)

Zophar's first Speech.

11 1 Then Zophar the Naamathite answered and said :

*To Zophar's mind the thought of Job not deserving all he suffers
is the merest blasphemy.   God affirms his guilt by his suffering.*

2 Must a mére stress of wórds go unánswered ?
    Must a bábbler be coúnted as ríght?
3 Shall thy brágging redúce men to sílence ?
    Shalt thou móck with nóne to sháme thee ?

*It is easy for you to be unconscious of your guilt ; but what if God
    took you at your word and revealed it in the light of His all-
    seeing Wisdom ?*

4 Thou mayst sáy, "My wáy^d is púre,
    And cléan have I béen in Thy síght."

d Kittel's
text

v. 20.   The versions suggest *the days of my age* or *my days and mine age.*
In any case the references to Ps. xxxix. should be carefully studied.   The
general sense is this :—"Even a slave is allowed his brief evening rest when
his work is done (vii. 2).   Just such a space is all I ask now that the day of
my life is closing."

5 But Óh that Gód would spéak,
  And ópen His líps agáinst thee,
6 And shéw thee wísdom's sécrets !

ᵃ ? Gloss   [Fór that true-wísdom is mánifold ;] ᵃ
  Then wouldst knów God remíts thy desérts.

Zophar pictures the inscrutable wisdom of God as ground of terror.
Though Job may know nothing against himself, yet the all-
searching light of God shews all.

7 Canst thou réach to the seárching of Gód ?
  Or attáin to Shaddái's perféction ?
8 Heíghts of héaven !—What cánst thou ?
  Déeper than Sheól !—What canst knów ?
ᵇ I.e. *of*   9 Its méasure ᵇ is lónger than eárth,
His wisdom   Bróader it ís than the séa !

This being so Job has no right to call His action in question.
Zophar has specially in mind Job's words in Chap. ix. 11 ff.

                10 Íf He should chánge and imprison,
ᶜ Cf.   And hold júdgement—whó can prevént ᶜ Him ?
chap.
ix. 12   11 For Hé knows mén who are wórthless,
                  Sees guílt without néed to consíder.
                12 But a wítless mán will learn wísdom
                  When a wíld ass's cólt is born mán.

v. 6ᶜ.   This line as it stands in the text is too long for the metre.   Zophar
means to say that God has not punished Job so much as his sins deserved.
The Septuagint reads somewhat differently.
  v. 12.   The form of the sentence suggests that Zophar is quoting a proverb.
He means to imply that his friend Job has about as much chance of learning
wisdom as the wildest animal has of becoming human.

*Zophar now falls into the style of the Alphabetical Psalms just as
Eliphaz and Bildad have already done (see pp. 12, 21) but,
whereas their allusions are rather to Ps. xxxvii., Zophar seems to
follow Ps. cxii. 7—10 with its abrupt transition to the fate of
the wicked.*

13 Now if thóu[a] wouldst sét thy heart ríght   [a] Emphatic
     And strétch out thy hánds unto Hím—

14 If guílt's in thy hánd, put it fár,
     Let not wíckedness dwéll in thy ténts :—

15 Thou wouldst thén lift thy fáce without-spót ;
     Wouldst be stéadfast and háve no féar[b].   [b] Cf. Ps. cxii. 7 ff.

16 Then thóu[c] wouldst forgét thy mísery,   [c] Emphatic
     As wáters gone bý wouldst remémber it,

17 And a lífe would aríse more than moón-bright,
     Thou shouldst sóar and becóme as the mórning ;

18 Thou shouldst trúst for that hópe is assúred ;
     Shouldst look roúnd thee and rést secúre ;

19 Shouldst lie dówn with nóne to affríght thee ;
     Yea, mány should séek thy fávour.

20 But the éyes of the wícked shall fáil[d] :   [d] Ps. cxii. 10
     No pláce of réfuge is léft them,
     Their one hópe the outbréathing of lífe !

Job's third Reply.

12 1 And Job answered and said:

*Job bitterly complains that, unless he had been so afflicted, his
" friends" would not have presumed to instruct him in matters
he knew so well.*

2 No doúbt but that yé are the péople,
     And wísdom must díe with yóu !

v. 20. The Passion Psalms remind us that the Righteous Man may have
to say, "Mine eyes fail for waiting upon God" (Ps. lxix. 3) and, "All refuge
has failed me" (Ps. cxlii. 4). But, in Zophar's thought this was only the
experience of the wicked.

3 I tóo, like yóu, have sénse;

ᵃ Gloss
from chap.
xiii. 2

[I nówise fall shórt of yóu :]ᵃ

Who ís there that cánnot talk thús ?

*It is hard that Job, who is crying to God in a heart-felt difficulty,
should on that very ground become a derision to his friends.*

4 He that cálls unto Gód for an ánswer,

ᵇ Lam.
iii. 14

Becómes to his friénd a derísionᵇ.

The júst and the úpright is derísion !

5 A tórch that is spúrned by the eáseful

Is fítted for stúmbling féet.

ᶜ Cf. Jer.
v. 27 f.

6 The ténts of róbbers prósperᶜ,

There is sáfety for Gód-provókers,

For the mán whose strong-hánd is his Gód !

*Job now returns to the thought of vv. 2, 3. A man does not need
any special wisdom to see the "power" of God in the works of
Nature.*

ᵈ The
brute
creation

7 Ásk now the béastᵈ, it will téach thee ;

And the fówl of the aír, it will téll thee :

8 Or spéak to the eárth, she will téach thee ;

And the físh of the séa will decláre it.

v. 3ᶜ. Literally, "With whom are there not (sayings) like these ?"

v. 4. Plato foresaw what the lot of a righteous man might be in an evil
world. *Repub.* ii. 361 E. Compare Wisd. ii. 13 ff.; Ps. xxii. 8. I suspect
that the third line of this verse was the comment of a later writer who had
in mind those passages in the Prologue in which Job is so often called
"blameless and upright."

On the text see Kittel's notes.

v. 5. An exceedingly difficult passage, as may be seen by comparing the
E.V. and R.V. I suggest that Job is quoting a proverb as though he would
say, "It is easy for a man who sits in comfort in his well-lighted room to
despise the poor light of a torch, but there may come a time when his feet
may stumble in the darkness and he may know its value."

v. 6. This verse, at first sight, seems out of place, but it expresses Job's
difficulty : he wants to feel, if he can, that God is just.

9 Whó knoweth nót by all thése
   That Jáhveh's hánd hath wrought thís ?
10 In Whose hánd is the sóul of all lífe,
   And the spírit of áll mankínd.

These proverbs of Bildad's (Chap. viii.) I bring to the
test of my own experience.

11 Dóth not the éar test wórds,
   As the pálate tástes its fóod ?
12 "With the áged"—forsóoth—"is wísdom,"
   "And léngth of dáys is understánding."

All that the friends have said about God's absolute
power is true; but how does it help ?

13 With Hím is wísdom and míght,
   To Hím belongs coúnsel and undérstanding.
14 He throws dówn and it cánnot be búilt ;
   He imprísons and nóne can unfétter.
15 He retáins the wáters, and they drý :
   Or He sénds them flóoding the eárth.
16 With Hím is stréngth and sound-wísdom :
   Léader, misléader, both Hís.
17 He léads away coúnsellors spóiled[a],   [a] Mic. i. 8
   And júdges He máketh fóols[b].   [b] Is. xliv.
                                                   25
18 He lóoses the bónd[c] of kíngs,   [c] Ps. ii. 3
   And bínds their loíns with a waístcloth.
19 He léads away rúlers spóiled,
   And overthróweth those fírmly-estáblished.
20 He remóveth the spéech of the trústy,
   And tákes away sénse from the áged.
21 He poúreth contémpt upon nóbles[d],   [d] Ps. cvii.
   And lóoseth the gírdle of the míghty.   40

vv. 21 ff.   It is impossible to read *vv.* 21, 23, 24, 25 without recognising
allusions to Ps. cvii. But how vast is the difference ! The Psalmist's constant
refrain is, "Let men thank Jahveh for His lovingkindness, and His wonderful

22 He disclóseth the déep-things of dárkness,
   And bríngeth-forth déath-gloom to líght.

ᵃ Ps. cvii.
33 ff.
23 He incréaseth nátions—and destróyeth them ᵃ:
   He spréadeth nátions—and léaveth them.

ᵇ Ps. cvii.
40
24 He depríveth earth's chíef-ones ᵇ of sénse;
   Makes them wánder ᵇ the tráckless wáste;
25 So they grópe in the únlit dárk,

ᶜ Ps. cvii.
27
   And He máketh them wánder like drúnkards ᶜ.

13 1 Behóld, all thís mine eye sées,
   Mine éar both héars and consíders it.
2 What yé know that Í know álso,
   I nówise fall shórt of yóu.

*But there is this difference between us—I, on my part, would like to
reason with God on the justice of His acts—You, on your part,
merely seek to cover difficulties with plausible words.*

3 But Í with the Almíghty would spéak,
   Would desíre to réason with Gód;
4 Whereas yé are daúbers of líes,
   Wórthless physícians the lót of you.
5 Woúld that ye whólly were sílent!
   Thát should be réckoned you wísdom.
6 Héar now thís my impéachment,
   And atténd to the pléa of my líps.

works for the children of men." But Job has not yet seen his way to such a
conclusion. He would rather have said, with Paracelsus:
             "'Tis hardly wise to moot
Such topics: doubts are many and faith is weak.
I know as much of any will of God
As knows some dumb and tortured brute what Man,
His stern lord, wills from the perplexing blows
That plague him every way;......
                         I know as little
Why I deserve to fail, as why I hoped
Better things in my youth."

7 For Gód^a, will ye spéak what is wróng?
  For Hím^a, will ye útter decéit?
8 Will yé be pártial for Hím?
  Will yé be pléaders for Gód?
9 Is it wéll when He séarcheth you oút?
  Cán ye decéive Him as mán?
10 Trúly Hé will convíct you,
  If yé accept pérsons in sécret.
11 Shóuld not His dígnity fríght you,
  And the dréad of Him fáll upón you?
12 Your máxims all próverbs of áshes!
  Your defénces defénces of cláy!

^a Emphatic

The friends here, probably, shew signs of being shocked at what they regard as the profanity of Job. This moves him to still bolder speech.

13 Be stíll, I would spéak, even Í,
  And let cóme on mé what wíll.
14 I táke my flésh in my téeth,
  And pút my lífe in mine hánd.
15 Ló, though He kíll me, I wáit not,
  But will árgue my wáys to His fáce.
16 Thís too should be míne for sáfety,
  That a hýpocrite ís not befóre Him.
17 Give díligent éar to my spéech;
  Let my státement énter your éars.

Job addresses God.

18 Behóld, I have státed my caúse;
  I knów it is Í that have ríght.

v. 12. *Proverbs of ashes.* A proverb, according to the Hebrew thought, sets forth truth in the well-ordered form of comparison. It is indeed a little parable. When Job speaks of *proverbs of ashes* he implies that there is no coherence, no correspondence with truth. God's judgement will bring this home (see xlii. 7).

19 Who ís there to próve me wróngᵃ?
    For thén I'd be sílent and díe.
20 Only spáre me two thíngs,
    Then I wíll not híde from Thy Présence.
21 Lift fár Thine hánd from óff me;
    And lét not Thy térror affríght me.
22 Then cáll—and Í will ánswer;
    Or Í speak and Thóu shalt replý.

*As there is no answer to this challenge Job continues
                in a more subdued frame.*

*Job asks what special grievous sins could have merited such sufferings.
    He is fully aware that he shares a sinful nature. But that
    would not, either in his own view or in that of his friends,
    account for his lot.*

23 How mány my faúlts and síns?
    My transgréssion, my sín, make me knów it.
24 Whý shouldst Thou híde Thy fáce,
    And cóunt me an énemy of Thíne?
25 Shouldst Thou hárass a dríven léaf,
    And the drý cháff pursúe?
26 That Thou decréest agaínst me bítterness,
    Making me héir to the síns of my yóuth.
27 For Thou séttest my féet in the clóg,
    And márkest áll my páths:
    Thou crámpest the sóles of my féet.

14 1 Mán that is bórn of a wóman!
    Short-líved and sáted with tróuble!
2 As a flówer he cómes—then is wíthered;
    He flíes like a shádow and stáys not.
    [And hé consúmes as róttenness;
    As a gárment éaten by móth.]

v. 2. In the Hebrew the words I have placed in brackets come at the
end of Chapter xiii. where they are clearly out of place.

3 Yet on súch Thou dost ópen Thine éye !

One like thís^a Thou dost bríng into júdgement !

4 Oh that cléan might cóme from únclean !

5 Not óne, if his dáys are detérmined.

The cóunt of his mónths is with Thée :

He can páss not the límit Thou mádest.

6 Look awáy and lét him be stíll,

To enjóy his days-énd as a híreling !

7 For there ís indeed hópe for a trée,

Though cút, it agáin may spróut,

And the shóot thereof wíll not fáil.

8 Though its róot may wax óld in the éarth,

And the stóck of it díe in the gróund,

9 At the scént of wáter it búds,

And prodúces its bóughs as when plánted.

10 But a héro^b díes and is próstrate,

Yea, mán expíres, and where ís he ?

11 As wáters all góne from a séa ;

As a ríver wásted and dríed ;

12 So mán lieth dówn, not to ríse ;

While the héavens exíst they awáke not,

Nor cán they be róused from their sléep.

*If another life were possible Job would contentedly wait in the grave
in full confidence that when God's anger was over He would
once more favour His creature.*

13 Oh wóuldst Thou but híde me in Sheól,

Wouldst secréte me till the pássing of Thy wráth,

Wouldst sét me a límit, then remémber me !

vv. 4—6. A difficult passage. The general sense might be paraphrased
thus, " Man's life is, alas, too short for perfection, Why then should he not
be permitted, what every slave has, a little respite when his day (of life)
is closing ? "

Margin notes:

^a See Versions

^b *strong-man*

3—2

14 [If a mán shall díe can he líve?]
   All the dáys of my wárfare I would wáit,
   Untíl my reléase should cóme.
15 Thou shouldst cáll—and Í would ánswer—
   Thou wouldst yéarn toward the wórk of Thine hánds.

The gleam of inspiration is past : Job falls back on
the sorrows of the present.

16 Whereas nów Thou dost númber my stéps:
   Dóst Thou not wátch o'er my sín?
17 My transgréssion is séaled in a bág
   And Thou fástenest úp mine iníquity.
18 Truly móuntain may fáll and crúmble
   And a róck may be móved from its pláce.
19 Wáters may púlverise stónes,
   But to flóod the gróund with its áfter-growth.
   [If a mán shall díe can he líve?]
   And the hópe of mán Thou destróyest.
20 Thou dost máster him whólly—he góes—
   Chánging his fáce and dismíssing him.
21 Should his sóns come to hónour, he knóws not;
   Be they húmbled, he dóth not percéive it;
22 But his flésh is in páin for himsélf,
   And his sóul for himsélf doth móurn.

v. 14ª. This line interrupts the sense. I suggest that its proper place is in *v.* 19 where it is required.

v. 15. The emphatic pronoun *I* suggests the readiness of glad response. Job feels that, somehow, even death may restore the lost fellowship with God.

v. 19. The word we translate *after-growth* signifies (in every other passage) *that which grows of itself* (Lev. xxv. 5, 11 ; 2 Kings xix. 29; Isaiah xxxvii. 30). The line in square brackets I have transposed from verse 14, where it is out of place. The general thought of the passage may be expressed thus : "In Nature death and destruction prepare the soil for new and richer life : but with *man*, Job thinks, it is not so. He has no second life and his death enriches the world with no after-crop." Compare Browning's *Cleon*.

SECOND CYCLE OF SPEECHES

Eliphaz's second Speech.

15 1 And Eliphaz the Temanite answered and said :

Eliphaz becomes bitter and regards Job as an enemy to religion.

> 2 Should a wíse man give vént to vain nótions,
>   And fíll his bélly with stórm-blast,
> 3 Réasoning with tálk without prófit,
>   And with wórds that can dó no góod ?
> 4 Yea, thóu destróyest relígion[a]
>   And impáirest meditátion with Gód.
> 5 Thine iníquity prómpteth thy móuth
>   While thou chóosest the tóngue of the cráfty.
> 6 Thine own móuth doth condémn thee—not Í
>   And thy líps bear wítness agáinst thee.

[a] Lit. *fear* (i.e. *of God*)

The aged Eliphaz is indignant that one so much younger than himself should dare to slight the "Wisdom" of the ages.

> 7 Wert thóu first Ádam bórn,
>   And frámed[b] befóre the hílls ?
> 8 In the Cóuncil of Gód didst thou héarken,
>   And absórb in thysélf (all) Wísdom ?
> 9 Whát dost thou knów that we knów not ?
>   Comprehénd, and it ís not with ús ?

[b] Cf. Prov. viii. 22 ff.

v. 4.   The emphasis is on the word *thou*; as though he had said, "It is men like you who are the real enemies to true religion." Since, according to Eliphaz, *fear* and *religion* are identical it follows that any man who, like Job, ventures to think for himself must be treated as a heretic.

v. 5.   Having proved Job to be a heretic he now concludes that he is dishonest !

Alas, it was not an enemy that did this, but a good and pious man, Job's own familiar friend whom he trusted !

10 Both gréybeard and áged are wíth us,
 One ólder in dáys than thy fáther.

*Eliphaz now alludes to his first speech which he
honestly intended to be kind.*

11 Are Divíne consolátions too smáll,
 And the wórd that déalt with thee géntly?
12 Hów thine héart doth misléad thee!
 Thine éyes how lófty^a they áre!

^a Prov.
xxx. 13

13 That thou túrnest thine ánger 'gainst Gód,
 And bríngest such wórds from thy móuth.

*Eliphaz again alludes to his first speech which had
seemed so conclusive to himself (see iv. 17 ff.).*

14 Hów should frail-mán be cléan?
 Can wóman-bórn be ríghteous?

^b *holy
ones*

15 Lo, He pútteth no trúst in His ángels^b,
 Nor is héaven cléan in His éyes,
16 Much léss one abhórred and fílthy,
 Mán that drinks sín like wáter!

*Eliphaz falls back on the tradition he loved, which, as we have seen,
finds its Biblical exponent in the Alphabetical Psalms, only, now,
he confines himself to the sad fate of the wicked.*

17 I shéw thee, héar me......
 For thát I have séen I reláte:—
18 (Thát which the wíse have tóld
 Not híding things léarnt from their fáthers;
19 To whóm the Lánd was sole-gíven
 When there pássed not a stránger amóng them.)

v. 12.   On the text see notes in Kittel's edition.
v. 16.   The words, no doubt, are general but are peculiarly unkind to a
man in Job's condition (cf. John ix. 34).
v. 17^a.   The line is too short in the text.   Possibly a word has fallen out.

20 "The wícked torménteth himsélf all his dáys,
   And féw are the yéars that are stóred for the týrant."

The terrors of an evil conscience.

21 There's a sóund in his éars (as) of térrors;
   While in péace the spóiler beséts him.
22 He trústs no retúrn through the dárkness:
   And he féels himself wátched by the swórd.

The man is haunted by imaginary terrors.

23 He wánders for bréad, "Where ᵃ ís it ?"
   He knóws that disáster's ᵇ at hánd.
24 Tróuble and ánguish affríght him;
. . . .
25 Becaúse he set hánd against Gód;
   Played the váliant agáinst the Almíghty:
26 Rúnning at Hím stiff-nécked,
   With the thíck of the bóss of his búcklers:
27 For he cóvered his fáce in his fát,
   And máde thick-fát on his flánks.

ᵃ Text
doubtful
ᵇ See
Sept.
Gloss
*day of
darkness*

*The words which follow shew that the enemy that has thus defied
   God is not so much an individual as a People.*

28 So he dwélt in désolate cíties ᶜ,
   In hóuses that nóne could inhábit,
   Which were fítted ónly for héaps.
29 Not rích nor with wéalth abíding,
   With no cróps that bénd to the éarth ᵈ.

ᶜ Cf. Ps.
cvii. 4

ᵈ Text
uncertain

v. 20. Another instance of lines of four beats to which I have called
attention in the first speech of Eliphaz (p. 10). I have here placed these
lines in inverted commas because they may possibly be a quotation from the
Wisdom literature which was so dear to Eliphaz.

v. 24ᵇ. This line we leave untranslated as the text is certainly corrupt.
The R.V. translates, "They prevail against him, as a king ready to the battle."

30 [He cánnot depárt out of dárkness]
     And the fláme shall wíther his bránches,
     And by the bréath of His móuth he depárts.

^a Pro-
bably a
later
addition

31 [Lét not the stráying trust vánity,
     For vánity becómes his requítal :]^a
32 Befóre his day cómes it is páid;
     So his bránch will nót be gréen,
33 He shéds unripe-grápe like the víne,
     And cásts, like the ólive, his blóssom.
34 The congregátion of the gódless is bárren,
     And a fíre consumes bríbery's ténts.

^b Cf. Is.
lix. 4

35 Sórrow-concéiving, sin-béaring^b !
     And their wómb frames déceit (for themsélves).

Job's fourth reply.

16 1 Then Job answered and said :

Job is grieved that his oldest friend should turn against him.

     2 Mány such thíngs I have héard :
       Ye are áll of you sórrowful cómforters !

^c See xv.
2

3 Can "wíndy wórds^c" have énd ?
     Or whát incites thée to make ánswer ?

v. 30. The words in square brackets seem to interrupt the sense and may possibly be misplaced. They seem to be a variant of *v.* 22^a. The *flame* is the lightning (cf. Ezek. xx. 47 [xxi. 3]). The *breath of His mouth* is the violent wind.

v. 34. There is a *congregation* that is fitted only for fire (Ps. cvi. 17 f.). This congregation is *barren*. There is, on the other hand, a congregation that is fitted for God, and, being in-dwelt by Him, bringeth forth much fruit. Since Eliphaz is still thinking of the barren fruit tree we may compare Jer. xvii. 5—8.

v. 35. Eliphaz ends as he had begun. Compare iv. 8 and v. 6 where these two words which we have translated *sin* and *sorrow* occur together in a similar context. His contention there was that if there is a *crop* of *trouble* there must have been a *sowing* of *sin*. In the present passage he inverts the order and introduces the thought of conception, exactly as in Ps. vii. 14—16, sin bringing forth its own likeness and becoming its own avenger.

4 Í too could spéak like yóu,
Were yóur soul in mý soul's stéad:
I could stríng old-sáyings agáinst you,
And sháke my héad[a] agáinst you:
5 I could stréngthen you só—with my móuth[b],
Unspáring in líp-consolátion!

[a] Ps. xxii.
7 (8);
Lam. ii. 15
[b] See
Sept. for
text

Job now speaks in a sadder tone; the word "unsparing" suggesting to him the unsparing nature of his pain which neither words nor silence can assuage.   God and man are against him.

6 If I spéak, my páin is unspáring;
If I céase, what jót of it léaves me?
7 But nów it[c] has máde me outwórn;
I am désolate, útterly wásted!
8 Emaciátion is cóme to be wítness,
And my léanness is rísen agáinst me!
[It testifies to my face.]

[c] I.e. *my pain*

Job's complaint against God should be closely compared with the parallel passages in the Book of Lamentations, where Israel is the speaker.

9 His ánger hath tórn and pursúed me[d];
He hath gnáshed at mé with his téeth.
Mine ádversary shárpens his éyes[e].
10 They have gáped upon mé with their móuth[f];
Have repróachfully smítten my chéek;
They assémble togéther agáinst me.
11 Gód gives me úp to the wórthless,
And cásts me on the hánds of the wícked.

[d] I.e. *with hatred*

[e] *at me*
[f] Cf. Ps. xxii. 13

vv. 7, 8. My translation of these verses is founded upon an emendation of the Hebrew text which I have defended in the *Journal of Theological Studies*, Oct. 1913.
    The line which I have placed in square brackets reads like an explanatory gloss. It does not suit the metre and is not required by the parallelism.

12 Péaceful I wás—and He bráke me;
    Took me úp by the néck and crúshed me.

ᵃ Lam.
iii. 12 f.

    Yea He sét me úp for His tárgetᵃ;
13 His árchers encómpass me róund;
    He cléaveth my reíns, unspáring;
    He poúreth my gáll on the éarth;
14 He bréaketh me bréach on bréach;
    He rúnneth on mé like a gíant.
15 I have clád my skín with sáckcloth,
    And have láid mine hórn in the dúst.
16 My fáce is defíled with wéeping,

ᵇ *Eyelids*

    And deep-glóom is ón my brówᵇ:
17 Becaúse of the no-víolence in my hánds,
    And (becaúse) that my práyer is púre.

*Surely my blood, like that of Abel, will cry from the ground for my
    Avenger. Yes—there must be One (in spite of friends' un-
    kindness) who will set me right in the sight of God and man.*

18 O éarth, cover nót my blóod,
    Let not spáce suffíce for my crý.
19 Yea, nów behóld in héaven,
    My wítness, my vóucher in the ský!
20 (Althóugh) my friénds are my móckers
    Mine éye drops téars to Gód;
21 That He pléad for a mán with Gód,
    And for són of mán with his neíghbour.

v. 17. The R.V. "Although there is no violence" is far too weak. The
Hebrew idiom *no-violence* implies the very antithesis of violence. The
same expression is used of the Suffering Servant in Is. liii. 9, "Because that
no-violence he did..." It is difficult to believe that the two passages are
wholly independent. Job claims that he is not merely an innocent sufferer
but that his sufferings are the consequence of his innocency.

After this gleam of inspiration Job returns to the sad experience of the present. It would have been better if Chap. xvii. had begun here.

22 Surely féw are the yéars that will cóme,
Ere I gó whence is nó retúrn.

17 1 My lífe is consúmed, (and) my dáys;
Gráves are...'...fór me!

2 Áre there not móckers wíth me?
And mine éye must abíde their provókings.

Human friendship has failed, but Job once more appeals to God.

3 Pray be plédge for mé with Thysélf;
Who élse should strike hánds for mé?

4 For théir^a heart Thou hast hídden from wísdom;
Thérefore Thou wílt not exált them.

5 "Whoso repórteth^b his friénds for gáin,
The éyes of his chíldren shall fáil."

6 I am máde a býword of Péoples;
Am becóme a pórtent^c befóre them.

7 Mine éye is grown dím with vexátion,
And my mémbers are áll as a shádow.

^a I.e. *the friends'*

^b Jer. xx. 10

^c See Versions

The two verses that follow can scarcely have been spoken by Job. They probably represent the later comment of a pious writer.

8 The úpright are stónied at thís;
And the ínnocent is móved against the gódless.

v. 1. The metre requires some such division of the words, but the text is very doubtful, as may be seen from the Septuagint. The general sense seems to be that, though life is only sorrow, the privilege of death is denied him.

v. 4. *Thou wilt not exalt them,* i.e. to the high office of Mediator.

v. 5. This verse may possibly be a quotation from some familiar proverb.

v. 6. *A byword of Peoples,* i.e. not *a popular byword* but *a byword to the Peoples,* as in Ps. xliv. 14 (15). This would scarcely apply to Job as an individual sufferer but would be quite natural if the thought were of Israel as the Suffering Servant. Compare Is. liii.

9 Yet the ríghteous maintáins his wáy;
And the mán clean of hánds grows strónger.

Job now speaks.

10 But áll of you túrn now and cóme;
And I fínd not a wíse-one amóng you.

ᵃ I.e. *my*
fate

11 My dáys ᵃ have excéeded my síns;
The stríngs of my héart are bróken.

These friends of mine talk about a bright future rising
for me (xi. 15 ff.), but they know not what they say.

ᵇ See xi.
17

12 Níght they would máke into dáy ᵇ:
Dáwn they would pút for dárkness.

13 While I lóok for Sheól as my hóme,
Have spréad my cóuch in the dárkness;

14 Have críed to the Pít, "My fáther":
To the wórm, "My móther, and my síster";

15 Where thén is that "hópe" of míne?

ᶜ See xi.
18

"My prospérity ᶜ," whó will sée it?

16 Will it gó with mé to Sheól?
Descénd we to dúst togéther?

Bildad's second Speech.

18 1 Then answered Bildad the Shuhite and said:

v. 11. The structure of the verse requires this division. The Hebrew
scholar will see in Kittel's note a justification of the reading I have given in
the second line. But the text is uncertain.

vv. 15, 16. The Septuagint here gives the better text. See Driver's note,
and Kittel's critical text.

Job's satire is directed against the easy optimism of Eliphaz (v. 17—27;
xi. 13—19).

It is Job's place to listen, not to teach. Can he expect
that, in his case, the penalty will not follow the sin ?

2 When wílt thou set énd to wórds ?
   Shouldst pónder, and wé should spéak.
3 Why shóuld we be coúnted as brútes,
   And vílely estéemed in your éyes ?

4 [One that téareth his sóul in his ánger]ᵃ
   Must for thý sake the éarth be forsáken ?
   And the Róckᵇ be remóved from His pláce ?
5 Yea, the líght of the wícked ís quenched ;
   And the fláme of his fíre shall nót shine.
6 Líght grows dárk in his tént ;
   And his lámp abóve him goes oút.
7 The stéps of his stréngth are stráitened,
   That coúnsel of hís casts him dówn.
8 He was lóosed with a nét round his féet,
   And góes abóut upon nét-work.
9 A gín shall lay hóld on his héel,
   A snáre shall be fírm upón him.
10 A nóose for him híd in the gróund,
   A tráp for him sét in the páth.
11 Térrors affríght him all roúnd,
   And cháse him hárd at his héels.
12 His stréngth shall píne awáy,
   And calámity shall be réady for his hálting.

ᵃ Line
misplaced

ᵇ I.e. *the
Creator*

v. 2. The reading of the Septuagint is here to be preferred. See Kittel
for Hebrew text.
v. 4. The line in square brackets does not suit either the context or the
structure of the verse.
vv. 7 f. The idea of the man being cast down by his own plans gives rise
to the picture in *v*. 8 of an animal let loose with a net round its feet. Bildad
spins out this thought in the verses that follow.

13 Dread-diséase shall devóur his límbs,
   It devóurs the mémbers of his bódy.
ᵃ See
Sept.
ᵇ I.e. *to
judgement*
14 Héalthᵃ is upróoted from his tént,
   And térror doth hául him to the kíngᵇ.
15 It dwélls in his hóme, unhóming it,
   Brímstone is scáttered on his dwélling.
16 His róots down belów shall be dríed,
   And his shóots up abóve shall be wíthered.
17 His memórial is pérished from éarth,
   No náme is hís in the stréet.
18 They thrúst him from líght into dárkness,
   And húnt him oút of the wórld.
19 No kíth or kin léft 'mid his Péople,
   Nor survívor thére where he sójourned.
ᶜ Lit. *day*
20 The Wést is amázed at his fáteᶜ,
   And théy of the Eást are in térror.
21 Yes, súch are the dwéllings of wíckedness,
   Such the pláce of the Gód-deníer.

Job's fifth Reply.

19 1 And Job answered and said :

*If I were suffering the consequences of my sin surely that were
the ground rather for sympathy than for reproach from you.*

2 How lóng will ye véx my sóul,
  And bréak me in piéces with wórds ?
3 These tén times ye pút me to blúsh,
  Unashámed ye déal with me hárdly.

v. 13.   Bildad alludes to Job's leprosy, just as Eliphaz had done in xv. 16.
v. 14.   The Hebrew reads "His confidence," but the reading of the Sept.
"Health" is better.
   The Septuagint also suggests the interpretation I have given to the second
line of this verse.
v. 15.   Literally, *It dwells in his home so that it is not his,* i.e. so that the
home is no longer a home.   But the text is possibly corrupt.

4 Now trúly, suppóse I had érred ?
   With mysélf must abíde mine érror.
5 Should yé then vaúnt agáinst me,
   And pléad my repróach agáinst me ?

But, in point of fact, the error is not mine but God's.

6 Knów now, it is Gód that hath wrónged me,
   And hath cómpassed me roúnd with His nét.
7 Ló I cry, "Wróng !"—but unánswered :
   I cry loúdly, but jústice is nóne.
8 He hath hédged^a up my wáy, so I páss not,
   Dárkness He séts on my páths.
9 He hath strípped my glóry from óff me
   And táken the crówn^b from my héad.
10 He hath bróken me roúnd,—I am góne ;
   He hath móved my hópe like a trée.
11 He hath kíndled His ánger agáinst me
   And hath coúnted me (óne) of His énemies.
12 His tróops come ón all togéther
   And bánk up their wáy agáinst me,
   And encámp all roúnd my tént.

^a Lam. iii. 7, 9

^b Lam. v. 16

The exceeding bitter cry of a tender heart that finds
*   no human sympathy in its deepest need.*

13 He hath máde my bréthren dístant,
   Mine acquaíntance are whólly estránged.
14 My néarest and déarest have fáiled,
   They that dwéll in my hóme have forgótten me.
15 My máidens accóunt me a stránger,
   An álien I becóme in their éyes.

v. 12. The third line in this verse reads like a gloss. The Septuagint read only two lines.

vv. 14, 15. The metre requires this division of the words, and it is also suggested in Kittel's critical text.

16 My sérvant I cáll—he replíes not,
     I must (deígn to) entréat him with my móuth.

17 My bréath is stránge^a to my wífe,
     I am lóathsome to the chíldren of my bódy.

18 The mérest bábes^b despíse me,
     Should I ríse they would spéak agáinst me.

19 My íntimates áll abhór me,
     And súch as I lóved turn agáinst me.

20 My bóne cléaves to my skín
     And I 'scápe by the skín of my téeth.

21 Píty me, píty me, my fríends,
     For the hánd of Gód hath toúched me.

22 Why should yé, well as Gód, pursúe me,
     And néver be sáted with my flésh ?

*Out of this deepest pit of sorrow Job sees, for one brief
moment, a new Light in Heaven.*

23 Oh wóuld now that théy were wrítten !
     That my wórds were inscríbed in the bóok !

24 With a pén of íron and with léad,
     Engráved in the róck for éver !

And these are the words.

25 I knów my Redéemer is Líving

     And will stánd the lást upon éarth^c.

v. 25. The *Goêl* was originally the *next of kin* who had the right to *redeem*
the inheritance and to act as the *avenger of blood*. But in the times of the
Second Isaiah the word was constantly applied to God as the *Redeemer* of
Israel (Is. xli. 14; xliii. 14; xliv. 6, 24; xlvii. 4; xlviii. 17; xlix. 7, 26; liv. 5,
8; lix. 20; lx. 16; lxiii. 16).

It is in this sense that Job uses the word. Already (xiv. 13—15) he has
touched upon this thought. The injustice of the present drives him to the
thought of a future when God must take his part and be seen as his Redeemer.

When he says that this Redeemer will *stand the last upon earth* he does
not merely mean that *He will stand at last upon earth* but rather that this Redeemer or Avenger will *stand the last*, all enemies being subdued, *upon earth*.

26 Though my bódily-tént be destróyed,
   Yet apárt from my flésh I see Gód:
27 Whom Í shall behóld as míne,
   And mine éyes shall sée (Him) no stránger.
   Such hópe is summed úp in my bósom[a].   [a] See Vulg.

Beware lest this Avenger of mine condemn you.

28 Though ye sáy, "Whereín can we 'pérsecute'[b],   [b] See *v.* 22
   Since the róot of the mátter's in hím";
29 Yet féar for yoursélves from the swórd,
   So ye knów that there ís a Júdge.

Zophar's second Speech.

20 1 Then answered Zophar the Naamathite, and said:
   2 "Not só," do my thóughts respónd[c];   [c] Sept.
   And hénce is the háste that is ín me.
   3 For repróof that would sháme me I héar,
   So my spírit in wísdom makes ánswer.

*Job has had his prosperity: but the prosperity of the
wicked is brief.*

4 Knówst thou not thís of old tíme,
   Since mán was pláced upon eárth,

vv. 26, 27. The text is difficult and the Versions vary considerably.

My translation is based upon some emendations which I have suggested
in the *J.T.S.* Oct. 1913.

My bodily-tent. Lit. *my skin.* We may compare 2 Cor. v. 1, 4 with
Wetstein's note.

Whom I shall behold as mine, i.e. *as on my side.*

And mine eyes shall see (Him) no stranger, i.e. *not hostile.* Job had timidly
expressed this hope in xiv. 13–15 but now it comes to him with the certitude
of a new revelation.

v. 29. This verse has a supernumerary line which, literally translated,
would run thus: *Because (there is) wrath the punishments of the sword.* I believe
this to be a double gloss on the first line of the verse, thus:—*Yet fear for
yourselves* (Gloss *Because there is wrath*) *from the sword* (Gloss *the punishments
of the sword*).

5 That the sóng of the wícked is shórt,
And the jóy of the gódless but bríef?
6 Though his lóftiness moúnt to the héaven,
And his héad should réach the clóud;

7 While jóying[a] he périshes útterly:
Those that sée him do sáy, "Where ís he?"
8 He flíts as a dréam unrecóvered,
Is dispélled as a vísion of níght.
9 Eýe doth sée him no lónger,
And his pláce behólds him no móre:
10 His chíldren pay córt to the féeble[b],
Their hánds restóring his wéalth.
11 While his bónes are fúll of vígour,
All líes with hím in the dúst.

It is vain for him to hide his wickedness from men.

12 Though évil be swéet in his móuth,
So he híde it únder his tóngue,
13 Spáring not létting it gó,
And kéeping it stíll in his móuth,
14 Yet his fóod túrns in his stómach,
Poíson of ásps withín him.
15 The wéalth that he swállowed he vómits,
God cásts it fórth from his bélly.
16 He súcks the gáll of ásps;
The tóngue of the víper sláys him.
17 He shall not lóok upon flóods,
Stréams of hóney and cúrd.
18 Fruit of tóil he restóres without tásting,
As wéalth given báck unenjóyed.
19 Since he crúshed the stréngth (?) of the póor,
Took by fórce the hoúse that he búilt not.
20 Since he néver knew rést withín,
He saves naúght of thát he desíred.

a See
Sept.

b Text
doubtful

21 From his méal there was nóthing left óver ;
   So prospérity cánnot stay with him.
22 In fúll self-sufficiency he is stráitened ;
   Each hánd brought to wóe is agaínst him.

It will be impossible for him to escape, for all creation
conspires to punish him.

23 When he fáin would fíll his bélly,
   God cásts upón him His wráth.
   [Lets it raín upon hím for his fóod.]ᵃ   ᵃ ꝺ Gloss
24 Though he flée from the wéapon of íron,
   The bów of bráss strikes him thróugh.
25 Drawn fórthᵇ it comes oút of his bódy ;   ᵇ I.e. *the*
   Yea, the glíttering-poínt through his gáll.   *arrow*
   The térrors (of déath) inváde him ;
26 All dárkness is stóred for his tréasure.
   A fíre unblówn shall devóur him,
   Shall sweep óff what is léft in his tént.
27 The héavens revéal his guílt,
   And eárth itself ríses agaínst him.
28 The incréase of his hoúse shall depárt,
   Flowing óff in the dáy of His wráth.
29 Such the wícked man's pórtion from Gód,
   His divínely appoínted héritage !

Job's sixth Reply.

21 1 And Job answered and said :

The friends may speak (xv. 11) of "Divine Consolations," but Job's
trouble is that he cannot reconcile the facts of life with the
justice of God.

   2 Give éar, give éar, to my spéech,
     And let thís give you gróund for "consólement "ᶜ.   ᶜ Chap.
   3 Permít me, for Í too would spéak ;   xv. 11
     Then, whén I have spóken, mock ón.

4 As for mé, is it mán I complaín of ?
   So whý should I nót be impátient ?
5 Atténd to my cáse, and be dúmb,
   And láy your hánd on your móuth.

This injustice of God fills me with wonder and dismay.
6 When I cáll it to mínd I am mázed,
   And hórror takes hóld on my flésh.
7 Why ís it the wícked do líve,
   Grow óld and wax míghty in pówer ?

All that the "friends" have said about God's judgements on the
wicked is contradicted by the plain experience of life.
8 Their séed is estáblished befóre them,
   And their óffspring befóre their éyes.
9 Their hóuses are péace without féar,
   And nó rod of Gód is on thém.
10 Their búll doth génder unfáiling ;
   Their ców doth cálve without míssing.

^a Cf.
chap.
xix. 18
11 They sénd forth their yoúng^a like a flóck,
   And their chíldren skíp (like lámbs).
12 They táke up the tímbrel and hárp,
   And rejoíce at the soúnd of the pípe.

They have an easy life and an easy death (cf. ix. 23).
13 They spénd their dáys in prospérity,

^b Or, *in*
qutet
   And go dówn to the gráve in a móment^b ;
14 Having saíd unto Gód, " Depart fróm us ;
   We desíre not to knów Thy wáys.
15 Whát is Shaddái that we sérve Him ?
   What gaín have we práying to Hím ?"

^c I.e. *in*
their power
16 Their prospérity ? is it nót in their hánd^c ?
   Far from mé is the coúnsel of the wícked.

v. 16. Their own strong hand is their god. Job is tempted almost to the
verge of atheism by the prosperity of the wicked. His position is that of the
Psalmist in Ps. lxxiii. 12–14. But he has not yet found a solution.

But though Job does not defend the life led by the wicked, yet he sees
that what Bildad has said about their " light being put out"
(xviii. 5 ff.) is contrary to fact.

> 17 Is it óft that their lámp^a is put oút,
> Their calámity cóming upón them,
> Those paíns He assígns in His ánger ?
> 18 Aré they as stráw before wínd ?
> As cháff swept awáy by the stórm^b ?

^a *lamp of*
the wicked

^b Ps. i. 4

But you evade this difficulty by asserting that the punishment
comes on the wicked man's children. You say,

> 19 " God stóres his guílt for his chíldren."

I reply,

> Let Him páy the man's sélf that he knów it.
> 20 Let his ówn eyes sée his calámity ;
> Let him drínk of the wráth of Shaddáī.
> 21 For whát concerns hím in his hoúse^c
> When his ówn tale of mónths is cut shórt ?

^c I.e. *his*
family

To this you will answer with your old argument that God is too high
for us to understand Him. But that does not satisfy me. You
say,

> 22 " Shall ány teach knówledge to Gód ?
> Seeing Hé judgeth thóse that are hígh."

I answer that it is terrible to feel God to be unjust : but when
I look at life what do I see ?

> 23 Here is óne who díes in full stréngth,
> Being whólly at eáse and quíet :
> 24 His lácteal véssels are fúll,
> And the márrow of his bónes is moístened.

v. 21. The text has *in his house after him,* but though this gives the sense
the words are too many for the metre. I therefore regard *after him* as a
gloss.

ª *in bitter-*
ness of soul

25 Anóther díes broken-heártedª
   Without éver tásting of góod.

26 Both alíke lie dówn in the dúst,
   And wórms do cóver them óver.

Of course you will say that if we could see the hearts of these two
men their several fates would be accounted for, and thus you
would imply that my sad fate proves my guilt.

27 Behóld I knów your thoúghts ;
   The devíces wherebý ye wróng me.
28 (Ye would say,)
   " Whére is the hoúse of the nóble ?
   And whére is the tént of the wícked ? "

You think that the former stands firm and the latter is removed,
but experience points just the other way.

29 Háve ye not ásked of trávellers ?
   And wíll ye not nóte their tókens ?
30 That the wícked is spáred in calámity,
   Drawn awáy in the dáy of wráth ?
31 Who télleth his wáy to his fáce ?
   Who requíteth the íll he has dóne ?
32 Yet hé is bórne to the sépulchre,
   And wátch is sét o'er the píle.
33 Sweet for hím are the clóds of the válley ;
   While áfter him áll men dráw.

vv. 32 f. These words describe the pomp of the tyrant's funeral and
should be closely compared with Ps. xlix. 11–13. The success of such men
encourages others in evil.

v. 33. The world would, in its servile homage, make corruption itself
sweet for him.

If you were honest you would confess that this is true.   Why then will you persist in speaking as though goodness were always rewarded by prosperity ?

34 How cómfort me thús with vánity,
   When your ánswers léave only tréspass ?

THIRD CYCLE OF SPEECHES

Eliphaz's third Speech.

22 1 And Eliphaz the Temanite answered and said :

Eliphaz in both his previous speeches has maintained that no man can be just before God (iv. 12 ff. ; xv. 14 f.).   He now meets Job's desire to argue his cause with God (xiii. 3 ; xiv. 22 f. ; xvi. 21). This, he says, is unreasonable.   Job must not expect God to justify His judgements by saying, " You have done this and that thing that was wrong."

2 Can a mán bring prófit to Gód ?
   The wíse doth but prófit himsélf.
3 Can Shaddáï in thy jústice be ínterested,
   Or gáin when thou wálkest upríghtly ?
4 Through féar of thée will He árgue ?
   Will He énter with thée into júdgement ?

   Saying,
5 " Ís not thy wíckedness gréat ?
   Thine iníquities áre they not éndless ?
6 Without caúse didst take plédge of thy bróther,
   And didst stríp the náked of clóthing.

v. 34.   Job does not mean that in their answers " there remaineth (only) falsehood " (R.V.), but rather that the only conclusion that can be drawn from their answers is to impute trespass to himself.

7 No wáter didst gíve to the wéary,
   Didst withhóld (thy) bréad from the húngry.

Thou didst act as a tyrant : thy motto was,

ᵃ Cf. Is.
v. 8

8 The lánd belóngs to the stróngᵃ,
   And mén of ránk should dwell ín it.

9 Didst sénd away émpty the wídow,

ᵇ Sept.
and Vulg.

   And didstᵇ bréak the árms of the fátherless.

10 Thérefore (these) snáres are all róund thee,
   And pánic féar dismáys thee.

ᶜ Sept.

11 Thy líghtᶜ is dárkened past séeing,

ᵈ Cf.
chap.
xxxviii.
34

   And abúndanceᵈ of wáters do cóver thee."

But though you, Job, must not expect God to explain to you His actions, yet neither, on the other hand, must you think that He dwells in heaven, careless of mankind. To do so would be to imitate the sinners who were destroyed by the Flood.

12 Ís not Gód in high héaven ?
   The tópmost high stárs He behólds !

13 And thou sáyest, " Whát doth God nóte ?
   Cán He discérn through the dárkness ?

14 With the clóuds as His cóvert He sées not ;
   While He wálks on the váult of the héaven."

15 Wilt thou kéep to that wáy of old tíme,
   Whereín the wícked men wálked

16 Who were shrívelled befóre their tíme,
   When the flóod overwhélmed their foundátions ;

vv. 12–18. Eliphaz here alludes to Job's words in xxi. 13–16 as though he would say, " So far from sinners having an easy life and an easy death, look at the generation of the Flood and learn therefrom that God is not regardless of mankind. You, Job, say *Far from me is the counsel of the wicked* (xxi. 16), I quite agree with you, and I repeat the same words, for your benefit, since you think of God as not regarding. That is the ' old way ' of atheism."

v. 16. There is probably an allusion to the Flood, but it is possible to translate *Their foundation was poured out (like) a river.*

17 Who saíd unto Gód, "Depart fróm us";
    And, "Whát can Shaddái do to ús?"
18 Though He fílled their hoúses with góod!
    Far from mé is the coúnsel of the wícked!

This proof of the judgement of God is a comfort to the righteous.
A cold-blooded thought quite in keeping with Eliphaz's theology.

19 The ríghteous sée and are glád;
    And the ínnocent láugh them to scórn:
20 "Ís not their súbstance (?) destróyed?
    And a fíre hath consúmed their wéalth."

Eliphaz concludes, as usual, with good advice : all true,
but all futile.

21 Confórm now to Hím, and have péace:
    Therebý there shall cóme to thee góod.
22 Accépt from His moúth instrúction,
    And láy up His wórds in thine héart.
23 If thou túrn to Shaddái thou shalt édify[a];   ^a *be built*
    If thou pút away wróng from thy tént: *up*
24 Setting góld on a lével with dúst,
    Ophir-góld as the stónes of the bróoks;
25 So Shaddái becómes thy góld,
    And sílver of wórth to thée.
26 For só, in Shaddái, thou shalt glóry,
    And shalt líft up thy fáce unto Gód.
27 Thou shalt práy unto Hím, and He héars thee;
    And só thou shalt páy thy vóws.
28 The thíng thou decréest shall stánd,
    And líght shall shine fórth on thy wáys.
29 When abásed thou shalt sáy, "Exaltátion";   ^b Cf.
    Him lówly of éyes will He sáve[b].   Prov.
                                                     xxix. 23

vv. 29 f.   The text is corrupt, but the Versions enable us to determine the
general sense.

30 He delívers the mán that is ínnocent ;
Thou shalt 'scápe through thy cléanness of hánds.

Job's seventh Reply.

23   1 And Job answered and said :

*The heartless incapacity of Eliphaz drives Job, all the more, to God.
He feels that God would not treat him so, if only he could meet
Him face to face.*

2 Of a trúth now, my plaínt is bítter,
But His hánd outweíghs my gróaning.
3 Woúld that I knéw where to fínd Him !
I would cóme even úp to His séat :
4 I would láy my caúse befóre Him,
And fíll my móuth with árguments.
5 I would nóte the wórds He would ánswer,
Would understánd what, to mé, He would sáy.
6 Woúld He with pówer impléad me ?
Náy ; He would gíve me héed.
7 There úpright, though stríving with Hím,
I should frée myself quíte from my júdge.

*So far from being an atheist (xxii. 12 f.) Job's whole heart goes
forth to find God ; and his conscience is free from guilt.*

8 Behóld I go Eást—but He ís not !
And Wést, but I cánnot percéive Him ;
9 On the Nórth, when He wórks, I behóld not :
I túrn to the Sóuth, but I sée not.
10 But He knóweth the wáy[a] that is wíth me ;
Had He tríed me, I had cóme forth góld.

[a] I.e. *my
course of
life*

v. 30. Again the text is impossible. The reading of the R.V. suggests
that even those who were not innocent would be delivered at Job's intercession. But such a thought is here quite out of place, and has no support
from the Versions. The speech of Eliphaz undoubtedly ended with a pious
platitude.

11 My fóot hath held clóse to His stéps ;
   His wáy I have képt unswérving.
12 From the láw of His líps I depárt not ;
   I have tréasured His wórds in my bósom[a].   ^a Sept.

*Job's love of God is rooted in the past ; but this makes it only the
more hard for him to understand God's strange dealings with
him in the present. Job's truthfulness makes him seem in-
consistent.*

13 But Hé is the One[b],—who can túrn Him ?   ^b ? Text
   What His sóul doth desíre that He dóeth.
14 Thús He will fínish His púrpose,
   And óther like thíngs are His mínd.
15 This is whý I'm dismáyed befóre Him ;
   When I pónder, of Hím I'm afráid.
16 For 'tis Gód who hath wéakened my héart ;
   And Shaddā́i who hath caúsed me dismáy.
17 For I am nót cut óff through the dárkness ;
   Nor for glóom that hath cóvered my fáce.

24 1 By Shaddā́i no séasons[c] are stóred ;   ^c I.e. *of
   They that knów Him do nót see His dáys.   vengeance*

v. 16. The names of God in this verse, *Él* and *Shaddā́i*, are significant.
El, the *Strong-God*, hath shewn His strength by weakening my heart !
Shaddai, the *Abundant-giver*, has abundantly caused me dismay !

v. 17. The rare word here translated *cut off* occurs in the saddest of all the
Psalms, Ps. lxxxviii. 16, *Thy terrors have cut me off.* See context. This is
exactly the thought in Job. " Job is overwhelmed, not by his calamity itself
(' darkness,' as in xv. 22 ; xvii. 12), but by the unjust providence to which it
seems to him to be due " [Driver].

In the case of Job (as in Ps. lxxxviii.) the deepest sorrow was this hiding
of God's Face.

vv. 1, 2. The first member of *v.* 1 has, in the Hebrew, a word too much for
the metre ; while the first member of *v.* 2 has a word too little. I propose to
omit the word translated *Why* in the R.V. from *v.* 1 and to replace a very
similar word, which can be translated *the wicked*, in *v.* 2, where the Sept.
actually reads *the wicked*.

ᵃ So Sept.

2 [The wícked] remóve the lándmarks ;
   They rób the flóck with the shépherdᵃ.
3 They dríve off the áss of the fátherless ;
   Take the wídow's óx for a plédge.
4 The néedy they thrúst from the wáy ;
   So the póor of the lánd must all híde.
5 Líke the wild-áss in the wílderness,

ᵇ Gloss
to their
work

   They gó forthᵇ séeking for fódder :
   The júngle is fóod for his yoúng-ones.
6 In a fiéld not their ówn they réap ;
   And gáther the víntage of the týrant.
7 They are náked all níght without clóthing ;
   No cóvering theírs from the cóld !
8 They are wét with the móuntain ráins,
   And embráce the róck for a shélter.

The verse which follows has evidently been misplaced. It refers to action of the oppressors and would naturally come after v. 3.

9 They stéal the fátherless from the bréast
   And take the bábe of the póor in plédge.

The context respecting the oppressed labourers is now resumed.

10 Náked they gó without clóthing,
   And while fámishing cárry the shéaves ;

Job's complaint, in *v*. 1, is that God allows wickedness to go unpunished so that those who reverence Him have no evidence of His justice.

v. 5. The words are so chosen as to keep the picture of the wild-ass in the mind. A vivid picture of the poor man's scanty earnings ! The words *to their work*, while they express the meaning, spoil both the metre and the poetry. We must regard them as an early prosaic gloss. It is possible indeed that the whole of the second line of the verse is a prose interpretation, the first and third lines suffice for the parallelism.

v. 6. The words *not his own* occur in xviii. 15. This is the meaning in the present passage. The R.V. reads the two words together and renders *his provender* but the Vulgate gives the right meaning.

11 In betwéen the two wálls they press óil ;
    The wíne-fats they tréad and are thírsting.

Job now passes in thought to the sorrows of the city.

12 From the cíty comes gróan of the dýing ;
    And the sóul of the wóunded cries óut.

13 Yet (since) Gód makes nó inquisítion,
    These cóme to be sínners 'gainst líght :

13ᵇ They récognise nót His wáys ;
    Nor dó they abíde in His páths.

14 The múrderer ríseth betímes ;
    [He would kíll the póor and néedy]
    And by níght the thíef goes róaming.

15 The adúlterer's éye waits the twílight,
    Sáying, "No éye shall sée me" ;
    And he púlleth a véil on his fáce.

16 In the dárk they díg through hóuses :
    By dáy they shút themselves úp.
    [They know not light.]

17 For mórning to thém is as déath-gloom,
    For they féel then the térrors of déath-gloom.

         *   *   *   *   *   *   *

         *   *   *   *   *   *   *

21 He devóureth the bárren that báre not ;
    And dóeth no góod to the wídow.

v. 13ª. According to the usual division into verses this would belong partly to *v.* 12 and partly to *v.* 13. The passage is one of extreme difficulty as may be seen from the Sept. which may possibly hint at Gen. vi. 4.

v. 14. The second member of this verse is commonplace and is, I suggest, an early gloss.

vv. 18–20. The text in these verses is so corrupt that any attempt at translation can only be misleading. The Hebrew gives neither sense nor metre and the Septuagint and Vulgate show that, in early days, no reasonable meaning could be found.

22 He dráweth the stróng through his pówer :
When he stánds, none trústeth to líve !

*But it is just these tyrants that God favours ; in
their life and in their death.*

ᵃ Lit. *are
upon*

23 Yet He gránts to such sáfety and péace ;
And His éyes (seem to) fávourᵃ their wáys.

24 Exálted—a spáce—then they áre not !
Brought lów—gathered ín—like the rést !
[They are cút like the tóp ears of córn.]

25 Now if nót, who will próve me a líar,
And máke my assértion wórthless ?

Bildad's third Speech.

*A portion of this Speech is, in the text, assigned to Job, thus
confusing the argument. We accept the suggestion of many
scholars and assign xxvi. 5—14 to Bildad.*

25 1 Then answered Bildad the Shuhite, and said :

2 Domínion and dréad are with Hím,
Making péace (as He dóes) in high-héaven,

ᵇ I.e. *the
stars*

3 Can His tróopsᵇ (on hígh) be númbered ?
And on whóm doth His líght not aríse ?

4 How can mán, then, be júst with Gód ?
How can wóman-bórn be cléar ?

5 Lo, the móon itsélf has no bríghtness,
And the stárs are not cléar in His éyes,

6 Much léss frail-mán, corrúption,
And the són of mán, a wórm !

v. 23. The text is by no means certain. My translation gives what
I believe to be the general sense. Safety in life, peace in death.

v. 24. They have power in life and carry all before them. True they
die, like all others, but their end is so easy that it seems rather like the
harvesting of ripe corn ! The word *gathered in* is used of the *ingathering* of the
fruits of the earth and probably suggested the third line of the verse which I
take to be an early gloss.

Job's eighth Reply, interrupting Bildad.

26 1 And Job answered and said :

2 How vástly thou aídest the pówerless !
Givest stréngth to the hélpless árm !

3 Dost coúnsel the óne without wísdom,
And téemest with knówledge so sóund !

4 To whóm hast thou tóld these sáyings ?
Whose bréath was it cáme forth from thée ?

Bildad continues.

5 The shádes are in pángs befóre Him,
The Séas and their dwéllers in dréad.

6 Sheól in His présence is náked,
And Abáddôn háth no cóvering.

7 He strétcheth the Nórth^a o'er the vóid,
And suspéndeth the eárth over nóthing.

8 Fólding the wáters in His clóuds,
So the clóud is not rént benéath them,

9 He fástens the frónt of His Thróne,
Spréading His clóuds upón it.

10 He márks out the boúnd^b on the wáters,
To the cónfines of líght and dárkness.

11 The píllars of héaven trémble,
And are mázed at Hís rebúke.

12 By His pówer He bráke the Séa,
By His wísdom He smóte through Ráhab.

^a The region of the Pole-star

^b horizon

v. 4. The word we have translated *sayings* is a late word, frequent in the Book of Job (thirty-four times), where it has occasionally a bad sense and is even translated *byword* in xxx. 9. Job means to imply that Bildad is a mere repeater of trite sayings.

v. 5. I adopt a slight alteration of the text suggested in Kittel's edition of the Hebrew.

v. 12. The Sea is personified like the Monster Tiamat in the Babylonian mythology where the smiting of Tiamat is a creative act by which chaos was reduced to order.

13 By His bréath the héavens are béauty ;
His hánd pierced the swíft-flying drágon[a].

[a] Is.
xxvii. 1

14 Lo thése are but párts of His wáys,
Mere whísper we héar abóut Him !
But the thúnder of His míght who can knów ?

27 1 And Job continued his discourse and said :

*Job now returns to his own sad case. It is not the question of God's
power but of His justice. Job maintains, by a solemn oath,
that he is not guilty of those sins that his friends would lay to
his charge.*

[b] Cf.
chap.
xxiii. 16

2 As God líves, Who depríved me of ríght[b],
And Shaddái Who embíttered my sóul—
3 For my life is whóle withín me
And the spírit of Gód in my nóstrils—
4 My líps do nót speak fálse,
And my tóngue tells nó untrúth.

[c] I.e. *that
you are
right*

5 While I líve I will nót grant you ríght[c],
Nor remóve mine ínnocence fróm me.

v. 13. The wind that beautifies the heavens is here pictured as the
breath of God. It is His hand that destroys the dragon of darkness.

v. 14. Many poets have expressed this thought, but none ever expressed
it in such compelling brevity.

Compare, for example, Kirke White :

" What does philosophy impart to man
But undiscovered wonders ?

.   .   .   .   .

She but extends the scope of wild amaze
And admiration. All her lessons end
In wider views of God's unfathomed depths."

v. 4. I.e. " When I assert that these sufferings are not the result of any
grievous sin."

v. 5. The Masoretic text, *God forbid that I should justify you till I die,* is too
long for the metre ; but if we omit the words " God forbid " the metre is right,
and we have just the expression that is required by the negative oath.

6 My ríghteousness hóld I, unflínching,
  My héart doth not bláme me one dáy.
11 I would téach you the méthod of Gód,
  Not concéaling the plán of Shaddái.
12 Lo, yé too, áll of you, sée it,
  Then whý deal ye útterly váinly ?

It is now Zophar's turn to speak ; and, though the text contains no
heading to this effect, the words and thoughts are obviously those
of Zophar and quite inappropriate on the lips of Job. This has
been recognised by many scholars ; I therefore print this
passage as

Zophar's third Speech.

7 Let mine énemy bé as the wícked,
  Mine oppónent ás the iníquitous.
8 For whát is the hópe of the gódless[a] ;
  When Gód requíreth his sóul ?
9 Does Gód then héar his crýing,
  When there cómeth upón him distréss ?
10 Will he glóry[b] thén in Shaddái ?
  Will he cáll upon Gód and be héard ?

[a] Gloss
though he
get gain

[b] Chap.
xxii. 26 ;
Ps.
xxxvii. 4.

vv. 11,12. I have ventured to place *vv.* 11,12 in this context where they 11
are needed. Job appeals to his friends to recognise the fact that he has lived
in all good conscience. They know this ; but they are more intent on
justifying God than on recognising facts. Job, on the other hand, is slowly
coming to the light because he refuses to "conceal" ways of God that he
cannot yet explain.

v. 10. *And be heard.* Lit. *So that God is intreated of him.* I adopt the
reading suggested by the Sept. See Kittel's text and compare chap. xxii. 26 f.
For só, in Shaddái, thou shalt glóry ....Thou shalt práy unto Him, and He héars thee.
The thought is confined to the present life and we must not read the future
into it. The point is, Will his prayer be heard ? The "friends" would have
said, "No, because he is a sinner." Job would have said, "No, whether
sinner or saint, his time has come."

Job had asserted the prosperity of the wicked (xii. 6 ; xxi. 7—12) ;
Zophar now contradicts this.

^a Gloss
from God
^b Gloss
from
Shaddāī
^c Cf. chap.
xx. 10

^d Ps.
lxxviii. 64

13 The wícked man's pórtion is thís^a ;
    The lót that týrants recéive^b ;
14 Should his chíldren^c grów—'tis for swórd ;
    And his óffspring is scánt of bréad ;
15 His rémnant unbúried in déath !
    While his wídows make nó lamentátion^d.

16 Though he píle up sílver as dúst,
    And stóre himself ráiment as cláy ;
17 He may stóre—but the ríghteous wéars !
    And the ínnocent sháre the sílver^e.

^e Cf. chap.
xx. 15, 18,
28
^f Cf. Is.
i. 8

18 He búilds like the spíder, his hóuse ;
    As a bóoth^f which the víne-keeper máketh.
19 Rích he lies dówn—never móre !
    He but ópens his éyes—and he ís not !

^g Cf. chap.
xx. 25

20 Térrors^g overtáke him like wáters ;
    By níght tempest stéals him awáy.

^h *Storm-*
wind,
chap. xv.
2

21 The blást^h takes him úp, and he góes ;
    And it swéepeth him óut of his pláce.
22 It húrls at hím without píty,
    Though he trý and trý to escápe it.
23 Men cláp their hánds at hím,
    And híss him óut of his pláce.

v. 13. Zophar had used almost identically the same words in chap. xx. 29.
v. 20. In direct opposition to what Job had said in chap. xxi. 17 f. but
in full agreement with Zophar's speech in chap. xx. 6–29. See marginal
references.

*Zophar now elaborates the point that he had maintained in his first
speech (xi. 7 f.) that it is "impossible by searching to find out
God" and that the only Wisdom that man can reach is to do His
will (xi. 13 ff.). With this object he first draws a picture of
what man can do in mining beneath the earth for precious metals
and stones.*

28   1 There is trúly a míne for sílver,
     And a pláce for refíning góld.
   2 Íron from the dúst may be táken,
     And brónze may be mólten from stóne.
   3 One pútteth an énd to dárkness,
     And séarcheth to útmost complétion
     The stónes of deep-dárkness and déath-gloom.
   4 He sínketh a sháft out of síght.
     Forgótten by évery fóot,
     They háng (?) (there) and swíng (?) far from mén.
   5 As for eárth, out of hér cometh fóod ;
     While únder 'tis túrned up as fíre.
   6 Her stónes aré the hóme of the sápphire,
     And álso of dúst of góld.

The miner's path.

   7 There's a páth unknówn to the vúlture,
     Unséen by the fálcon's éye :
   8 The sóns of príde[a] never tród it,
     Nor the fiérce-lion pássed therebý.

[a] young
lions

vv. 3, 4. Two very difficult verses. I would suggest that 3[a] should be read
with 4[a], 3[b] with 4[b], 3[c] with 4[c], thus making three verses instead of two ;
somewhat as follows :—*He putteth an end to darkness ; He sinketh a shaft out of
sight : And he searcheth to utmost completion Things forgotten by the foot. The
stones of deep-darkness and death-gloom That ..... and ..... far from men.* In
any case we must contrast 3[b] with xi. 7 where Zophar, using the same words
for *search* and *completion*, maintains the impossibility of searching out God to
perfection.

Neither hard rock nor flowing water hinders man's search.

9 He púts forth his hánd on the flínt-rock ;
   Overtúrneth the hílls by their róots.

10 In the rócks he cútteth him chánnels ;
   And his éye sees eách rare thíng.

11 He bínds the stréams from tríckling,
   And bríngeth hid-tréasure to líght.

Though man finds a way through earth and rock and water, he cannot find the way to Wisdom nor the home thereof. Nor is it, as the Babylonians suppose, in the great Deep beneath the Earth.

12 But Wísdom ? whénce is it fóund ?
   And whére is the pláce of understánding ?

^c See
Sept.

13 The wáy ª to it mán knoweth nót ;
   'Tis not fóund in the lánd of the líving.

14 The Déep saith, " It ís not in mé " :
   And the Séa saith, " It ís not with mé."

   Wisdom cannot be bought by earthly treasure.

15 Góld is not páid in exchánge,
   Nor sílver weighed oút as its príce.

^b *Ophir
gold*

16 'Tis nót to be válued with Óphir ᵇ,
   With précious ónyx or sápphire.

v. 11. *From trickling,* lit. *from weeping.* By diverting the course of the stream he stops even the trickling and so lays bare the river bed in his search for its hidden treasures.

The Sept. and Vulg. had, however, a slightly different text which we might translate *He searcheth the depths of the streams.*

See Kittel's Hebrew text.

vv. 12, 13. In each of these verses we have the two thoughts *whence ?* and *where ? Whence ?* in 12ª, corresponds with, *The way to it* in 13ª, while *Where ?* in 12ᵇ, corresponds with, *'Tis not found in the land of the living.* See also *vv.* 20, 23.

v. 14. In the Babylonian religion the Deep was the home of Wisdom.

17 Góld and gláss do not équal it ;
   Nor are jéwels of góld its exchánge.

18 No méntion of córal or crýstal :
   Above péarls is Wísdom's príce.

20 But Wísdom ? whénce is it fóund ?
   And whére is the pláce of understánding ?

21 For 'tis híd from the éyes of all líving,
   And concéaled from the fówls of the héaven.

22 Abáddon and Déath have sáid,
   "With our éars we have héard its rúmour."

23 The wáy thereto Gód understándeth,
   And Hé it is knóws its pláce.

24 For Hé it is lóoks to earth's énds,
   And sées the whóle under héaven.

25 When He máde a wéight for the wínd,
   And méted the wáters by méasure,

26 When He máde for the ráin a láw,
   And a wáy for the thúnder-flásh :

27 Thén did He sée and decláre her[a] ;   [a] I.e.
   He stáblished her, séarched her oút.   *Wisdom*

28 But for mán, relígion [b] is wísdom ;   [b] *fear of*
   Understánding is túrning from évil.   *the Lord.*
                                      Prov. i. 7,

v. 19.   We omit this verse since it is merely a variant of *vv*. 17[a] and 16[a].   29; ix. 10

vv. 20 ff.   Verse 20 is a repetition of *v*. 12.   The same two thoughts must be noted, (*a*) *Whence is it reached ?* (*b*) *Where is its home ?*

The first question is answered by *v*. 23[a], *The way thereto God understandeth*, and the second by *v*. 23[b], *And He it is knows its place*.

Thus *v*. 23 must be compared with *v*. 13.

Man cannot understand and know because he does not see the whole of any one thing.   God sees Creation and sees it as a whole (*v*. 24).

v. 28.   The Masoretic text of the first line is pure prose ; thus : *And He said unto man, Lo, the fear of the Lord, that is wisdom.*   The line is too long for the metre, but the variations and omissions in some MSS. help us to restore it.

Zophar returns to his original contention in chap. xi. 7 ff. viz. that God cannot be known and that, instead of seeking to understand, Job must turn from evil (cf. xi. 13 ff.).

Job's Soliloquy.

29 1 And Job continued his discourse and said :

Job recalls the happy past when his home did but testify
that God was well pleased with him.

2 Wóuld that I wére as of óld,
　As in dáys when Gód used to kéep me ;
3 When His lámp shined bríght o'er my héad ;
　By His líght I could wálk in dárkness.
4 As I wás in my frúitful[a] dáys,
　When my tént meant the fríendship of Gód ;
5 While yét Shaddái was míne,
　And my chíldren róund abóut me :
6 When my stéps were báthed in cúrd,
　And my tréading ran rívers of óil.

Job pictures the respect and reverence with which he
used to be greeted.

7 When I wént in the gáte by the Cíty,
　In the bróad-way I'd sét my séat :
8 The yóung hid themsélves when they sáw me ;
　While the óldest róse up and stóod.
9 Prínces refraíned from tálking,
　And láid the hánd on the móuth.
10 The vóice of nóbles was húshed,
　And their tóngue used to cléave to the pálate.

v. 4[b]. When my converse with God was like that of a familiar friend.
Had Job but known it he was all the dearer to God for this trial (see ch. ii. 3).
"Meek souls there are who little deem
Their daily strife an angel's theme."
v. 6[b]. The text in its present form is impossible. I have adopted an
emendation suggested in Kittel's text which suits the metre and preserves the
parallelism.
Job means to say that wherever he went he prospered.

[a] *days*
of my
Autumn

21 They heárkened to mé and did wáit,
　　They sílently wáited my cóunsel.
22 When I'd spóken they spáke not agáin,
　　So. my wórds might drópᵃ upón them.
23 Thus they wáited for mé as for raín,
　　They gáped (as the eárth does) for spríng-rain.
24 I would smíle if théy were despóndent (?)ᵇ
　　And the líght of my fáce they depréssed not.
25 I chóse out their wáy and sat chíef,
　　And abóde as a kíng in the ármy.

ᵃ Deut. xxxii. 2

ᵇ [Gloss *as one that comforteth mourners*]

*And this respect in which he was held was not the fear
of a tyrant but the love of a benefactor.*

11 The éar did but héar and it bléssed me ;
　　The éye did but sée and appróved me :
12 For I sáved the póor that críed,
　　The fátherless álso, the hélpless.
13 On mé came the bléssing of the wrétched :
　　And I gláddened the héart of the wídow.
14 Mércy clothed mé, I becáme it ;
　　My jústice was róbe and túrban.

Verses 21–25 have clearly been misplaced. I restore them to their natural context.

v. 24. Of the many interpretations that have been given of this difficult verse I adopt the one that seems to me to be least improbable : but I am by no means satisfied that the text is correct. The words, "As one that comforteth mourners" which, in the text, occur as a third line of *v.* 25 are there out of place. I suggest that they were introduced as a gloss to explain *v.* 24ᵃ.

v. 14. When the Hebrew words for *righteousness* and *judgement* come together the former often has the sense of *mercy* the latter of *justice*.

The first line of the verse might be literally translated, as in the R.V. margin, *I put on righteousness, and it clothed itself with me.* Job means to say that he was the very impersonation of mercy.

15 I becáme as éyes to the blínd,
    And féet I becáme to the láme.
16 To néedy ones Í was a fáther,
    And the cáse that I knéw not I séarched.
17 And I bráke the fángs of the wícked ;
    Yea, plúcked the spóil from his téeth.

*This being so, I trusted to find happiness on earth (cf. the same
thought in Pss. xli., xliv. 1—8). Deuteronomy had promised
this.*

18 So I thóught, "I shall díe in my nést,
    I shall múltiply dáys as the sánd^a :

^a Or, *the phoenix*

19 My róot is spread óut to the wáters,
    And the déw lies all níght on my bránch :
20 My glóry is frésh withín me,
    And my bów is renéwed in mine hánd."

*But instead of the honour that God's word promises I have found
contempt (note the same thought in Ps. xliv. 9 ff.).*

30 1 But nów they that móck me are thóse
    Yoúnger in dáys than mysélf ;
    Whose véry fáthers I'd spúrn
    To sét with the dógs of my flóck.

^b Text doubtful

2 The stréngth of whose hánds...^b
    Mén in whom vígour was períshed ;
3 Gaúnt with wánt and fámine !
    They gnáw the árid désert,
    The lánd^b (?) wáste and désolate.

v. 16. He was *considerate for the poor and needy* and therefore ought to
have inherited the promise. See Ps. xli. 1.
vv. 18–20. A possible allusion to the promise in Jer. xvii. 8. As though
he had said, God's promise to the good man runs, that "he shall be like a tree
planted by the waters, and that spreadeth out her roots to the river, and does
not feel it. when heat cometh, but its leaf is green &c."

4 They plúck salt-wórt by the búshes,
And the róots of the bróom are their bréad.

5 They are dríven fórth from the mídst,
Men shóut after thém as a thíef.

6 In cléfts most hórrid they dwéll,
In hóles in the eárth and in rócks.

7 Amóng the búshes they bráy,
They are húddled únder the néttles.

8 Sóns of the fóol and the námeless,
They are smítten oút of the lánd.

9 But nów I'm becóme their jést^a;
I ám unto thém as a bý-word^b !

10 They abhór me, they stánd far alóof ;
They spáre not to spít in my fáce.

^a *song,*
Lam. iii.
14
^b Cf. Ps.
xliv. 13 f.

And all this indignity that I suffer from man is in consequence of
the affliction wherewith God has afflicted me (compare Ps. xlix.
9 ff. and Lam. iii.).

11 Since He sláckened my córd^c and afflícted me
They cást off the brídle^d befóre me.

^c Or,
bowstring
^d I.e.
restraint

12 On my ríght they ríse, a low-bróod,
And cást up their wáys agaínst me.

13 They bréak up my páth,
They strípped off my gárment^e,
There is nóne to restráin^f them.

^e So Sept.

^f See
Driver

14 As thróugh a wide bréach they come ón ;
In the témpest's stéad they roll ín.

15 Térrors are túrned upón me ;
They cháse my hónour (?) as the wínd ;
And my wélfare is góne as a clóud.

16 My sóul is poured oút withín me ;
Dáys of afflíction fast hóld me.

v. 13. The text is corrupt and the three short lines do not suit the metre.
The Septuagint read quite a different text but failed to find any true solution.

17 My bónes rot from óff me by níght;
   My gnáwings néver céase.
18 My róbe is chánged by main fórce;
   It bínds me as the cóllar of my cóat.

^a Text
uncertain

19 [Gód]^a hath cást me in míre,
   I am líkened to dúst and áshes.

Hardest of all to bear is the cruel neglect of God.

20 I crý, but Thou ánswerest nót :
   I stánd, but Thou dóst [not] regárd me.
21 Thou art túrned to be crúel towárds me;
   With the míght of Thine hánd dost shew hátred.

^b I.e. *toss*

22 Dost táke^b me and dríve me on wínd,
   And méltest me oút of exístence.

^c Gen. iii.
19

23 I know wéll Thou'lt retúrn^c me to déath,
   And the pláce where all líving must méet :
24 Yet one strétches a hánd in fálling,
   And críes out for hélp in calámity.

Did not God promise that the man who considered the poor and needy should himself be delivered in time of trouble ? But my experience is just the contrary.

25 Did I nót bewáil the ill-fáted ?
   Did my sóul not gríeve for the néedy ?
26 When I lóoked for góod, there came évil;
   When I hóped for líght, there came dárkness.

27 My bówels are séething, and rést not;

^d Ps.
xviii. 5 (6)

   Dáys of afflíction assáult^d me.

v. 24. I have given the most probable sense of this exceedingly difficult verse. Job seems to say to God, " I know it is useless for me to cry to Thee; but still is there not an instinct that compels a falling man to put forth a hand in his fall ? "

28 I go dárkened, but nót by the sún :
     I ríse up and crý with my vóice.

29 I am cóme to be bróther to jáckals,
     And a (fít) compánion for óstriches.

30 My skín (peels) from óff me all bláckened,
     And my bónes are búrnt with héat.

31 So my hárp is túrned to moúrning,
     And my pípe to the wáil of wéepers.

*Job well knows the penalty of lust : but he has kept himself pure in
act and thought (Mtt. v. 28). Job's standard of morality is
the nearest that the Old Testament knows to that of the Sermon
on the Mount.*

31   1 A cómpact^a I máde with mine éyes ;   ^a *covenant*
     How thén should I gáze on a máiden ?

   2 What pórtion from Gód abóve ?
     What awárd from Shaddāi in the height ?

   3 Is it nót for the wícked, calámity ?
     And, for wróng-doers, stránge disáster ?

   4 Doth not Hé Himself sée my wáys,
     And númber áll my stéps ?

   5 Íf I have wálked with fálsehood,
     And my fóot hath hásted to fráud,

   6 [Let Him wéigh me in éven bálance,
     And let Gód take nóte of mine ínnocence.]

   7 If my stép turned asíde from the wáy,
     And my héart did fóllow mine éyes,
     And spót hath cléaved to mine hánds,

   8 May I sów and anóther éat^b ;   ^b Deut.
     May my próduce be róoted úp.   xxviii.
                                         30 ff.

v. 28^b. The text reads, *I rise up and cry in the congregation.* This is quite
unsuitable to Job's condition or to the context : but, by changing one letter,
we may read, *with the voice* instead of, *in the congregation.* See Kittel's text.

Job seems to refer to the curses denounced in Deuteronomy.   He admits their justice but he himself has not incurred them.

9 If mine héart hath been 'tíced after wóman,
And I lúrked at the dóor of my neíghbour,
10 Let my wífe be the sláve of anóther,
And let óthers bow dówn upón her^a.
11 [For thát were a héinous críme ;
An iníquity fít for the júdges.]
12 Let a fíre burn dówn to Abáddon ;
Let it róot out áll mine íncrease.

38 If my fiéld cry oút agaínst me,
Its fúrrows all wéeping togéther,
39 If I áte of its stréngth without cóst,
Or shéd the lífe of its ówners,
40 Let thórns grow in pláce of whéat,
Vile wéeds in pláce of bárley.

Job has recognised the universal brotherhood of man.

13 If I spúrned the caúse of my mán^b,
Or máid, when they stróve with mé,
14 What thén should I dó when Gód rises ?
When He vísiteth, whát could I ánswer ?
15 Did not Hé that made mé make hím,
And fáshion him tóo in like^c wómb ?

^a Deut. xxviii. 30

^b *slave*

^c Lit. *one*

vv. 11, 12.   The metre is not correct in these verses, 11^a being too short and 12^a too long.   In the latter case it is fairly obvious that the words *For it* have been copied by mistake from the line above : I have therefore omitted them.

vv. 38–40.   I agree with many commentators in reading these verses in this context.

*Job has ever cared for the widow, the fatherless, the needy, because,
in them, he has seen God's image. (Compare the spirit of
Deuteronomy.)*

16 If I héld back the póor from their wísh,
   Caused the éyes of the wídow to fáil[a] ;

17 If I've éaten my mórsel alóne,
   So the fátherless áte not theréof ;

18 [Nay, he[b] gréw up with mé as his fáther,
   And hér[c], from my bírth, did I gúide.]

19 If I sáw any pérish unclóthed,
   Or the úncovered státe of the néedy ;

20 If the lóins of súch did not bléss me,
   When he wármed with the fléece of my lámbs—

21 If I ráised my hánd 'gainst the fátherless,
   Becaúse I saw hélp[d] in the gáte ;

22 Let my shóulder fáll from the bláde,
   And mine árm be bróken from the bóne.

23 For the féar of Gód was upón[e] me ;
   And I cóuld not becaúse of His dígnity.

*Job has been heart-free from "covetousness which is idolatry"
and from all the seductions of Nature-worship.*

24 If I (éver) made góld my cónfidence,
   And did sáy unto fíne-gold, " My hópe " :

25 If I jóyed that my súbstance was gréat,
   That my hánd had gótten abúndance :

26 If I sáw the líght when it shíned,
   And the móon as it wálked in spléndour,

27 And my héart was entíced in sécret,
   So my hánd went to kíss my móuth ;

28 That tóo were gúilt for the júdge,
   I had líed to the Gód abóve.

v. 23. It was not a craven fear of the consequences but a sense of God's
Presence. Cf. Gen. xxxix. 9, " How can I do this great wickedness and sin
against God ? "

a *with
longing*

b I.e. *the
poor, v.* 16
c I.e. *the
widow,
v.* 16

d I.e.
*friends at
court*

e See
Sept.

Job has been heart-free from malice.

29 If I'd jóyed at the fáte of my fóe,
    And exúlted when évil beféll him;
30 If I súffered my móuth to sín,
    By ásking his lífe with a cúrse :

Job claims that his hospitality was proverbial.

31 If the mén of my tént did not sáy,
    " Where is óne unféd with his fóod ? "
32 In the stréet no stránger did lódge ;
    I ópened my dóors to the tráveller.

Neither did the fear of man ever lead him to hide any wrong-doing.

^a ꝺ Gloss

33 If with mén I híd my transgréssion,
    [By concéaling my gúilt in my bósom,]ᵃ
    And kept stíll, not going fórth at the dóor,
34 Becaúse that I féared the great crówd,
    And contémpt of the cláns did affríght me.

Job is so sure of his innocence that he throws down, as it were, his gage before God, and challenges Him to answer.

35 Oh hád I but óne to héar me !
    (Lo, my márk, let Shaddāí give me ánswer ;)

^b indict-
ment

    Had I chárge ᵇ mine oppónent had wrítten !

v. 30. I have changed one little word, reading *If* (as in *vv.* 24, 25, 26, 29, &c.) instead of *And not.* Job has throughout claimed to have fulfilled not merely the letter but the spirit of the moral law. If the text stands we must translate, *And I suffered not my mouth to sin &c.* : this surely is something of a bathos after *v.* 29 ? Job could hardly have said that " he did not rejoice when evil happened to his enemy and *he did not even seek to kill him with a curse.*"

v. 33. Kittel's text (see also Sept.) suggests that the line which I have placed in square brackets is a gloss. I would further suggest that the words, *And kept still, not going forth at the door,* which occur as a third member of *v.* 34 (where they are meaningless) should properly form part of *v.* 33.

vv. 35–37. Though these words sound like rebellion they are, in very truth, the cry of a soul that would desire, above all things, to justify God but

36 I would béar it alóft on my shóulder ;
  As a crówn would I bínd it aróund me.
37 I would téll him each stép I had táken^a ;   ^a Lit. *the*
  Prince-líke would I dráw near befóre him.   *count of*
                                                      my steps

*The words of Job should end here.   But the text has the three verses
which would come much more naturally after v. 12 where I
have placed them.*

THE WORDS OF JOB ARE ENDED.

[The speech of Elihu[1] *(Chaps. xxxii—xxxvii) is, undoubtedly, a later
addition to the Book.   I have therefore placed these Chapters
in an Appendix so that the reader may be able to follow the
thought of the Poem in its original form.]*

38 1 And Jahveh answered Job out of the whirlwind and
        said :

   2 Who is thís that dárkeneth cóunsel
     With wórds without knówledge ?—
   3 Gírd now thy lóins like a mán ;
     I will ásk thee ; infórm Me, I práy.

is unable to reconcile the facts of life with the teaching of Deuteronomy.   No
doubt they were "words without knowledge" (xxxviii. 2) but they were
honest, and, as such, were more pleasing to God than the shallow orthodoxy
of the "friends" (xlii. 7).

v. 1. *Out of the whirlwind* (or *storm*).   Job was not yet ready for *the still small
voice*.   But though the words come from the storm they are charged with
compassion.   This is wonderfully brought out in Blake's *Vision of the Book of
Job* (Illustration xiii. Wicksteed's Edition) where the outstretched hands of God
seem to be lifting Job into the beatific Vision.

v. 2.   God does not accuse Job of sin but warns him that he is confusing
the issues of life by not regarding Creation as a whole.   This is not in-
consistent with the praise bestowed upon Job in chap. xlii. 7.

Earth implies a purpose.

4 When I fóunded the eárth, where wert thóu ?
Decláre if thou skíllest to knów.

5 Who appóinted her méasures ?   Dost knów ?
Or whó stretched the líne upón her ?

6 Her foundátions ?   On whát were they séttled ?
Or whó laid her córner-stóne ?

7 While the mórning-stars sáng in chórus,
And the sóns-of-God shóuted for jóy.

*The curbing of the Sea implies not merely the power of the
Creator but His good purpose towards man.*

8 Or whó shut the Séa up with dóors,
When it búrst and came fórth from a wómb ?

9 When I máde the clóud its vésture,
And dárkness its swáddling-bánd,

10 When I clénched on it Mý decrée,
And appóinted it bárs and dóors,

11 And sáid, "Thus fár shalt thou cóme[a],
And hére shall thy próud waves be stáyed" ?

ᵃ Gloss
*and no
further*

vv. 6 f.   Davidson quotes the *Hymn on the Nativity* :
  " Such music, as 'tis said,
  Before was never made,
    But when of old the sons of morning sung,
  While the Creator great
  His constellations set,
    And the well-balanced world on hinges hung ;
  And cast the dark foundations deep,
  And bid the weltering waves their oozy channel keep."

vv. 8–11.   In the Babylonian story the beginning of Creation was the
hard-won victory of Marduk over the Sea-monster, Tiamat, the personifica-
tion of Chaos : but here the Sea is God's little infant ; He clothes it with
clouds, wraps it in a swaddling-band and makes it obedient to His will.

A magnificent picture of the triumph of Light, and of the victory
of all good that is therein implied.

12 Didst thou éver give chárge to the Mórn,
   Or téach the Dáwn its pláce;
13 How to grásp the córners of eárth,
   Till the wícked be sháken thereoút?
14 She^a is chánged like cláy of a séal;   ^a I.e. *earth*
   Things stánd as though clóthed with a gárment;
15 While their líght is withhéld from the wícked,
   And the árm that is lófty is bróken.

The Under-world, a storehouse for good ends
beyond man's thought.

16 Hast thou éntered the mázes of Séa?
   Or wálked the recésses of the Déep?
17 Have, to thée, Death's gátes been revéaled?
   Hast thou séen the wárders^b of Hádes?   ^b Sept.
18 Canst thóu comprehénd to earth's boúnds?
   Declére if thou knówest it áll.

19 Whére is the wáy to light's dwélling?
   And dárkness? Whére is its pláce?
20 That thóu shouldst condúct it to boúnds,
   And shouldst knów the páths to its dwélling!
21 Dost thou knów it as béing then bórn?
   Is the númber of thy dáys so vást?

vv. 12–15. It would be difficult to find a more beautiful picture in the poetry of any language. The sudden sunrise filling the four corners of the Earth with light; bringing every hidden detail of beauty into the clear-cut outline of its own expression, thus becoming a daily parable of Revelation. But, more than this, the sunrise " shakes out " all wicked things that love not the light (*v.* 13); from these the benefit of light is withholden (*v.* 15); and thus we have a parable of the final extinction of evil (see the present writer's notes on Ps. civ. 22, 31–35).

God's treasure-house of snow and hail (see Pss. cxlvii. 16,
cxlviii. 8).

22 Hast thou éntered the stórehouse of snów ?
     And the stórehouse of háil, hast thou séen it ?
23 Which I kéep for the tíme of stréss,
     For the dáy of báttle and wár.

God's care reaches beyond man's ken.

^a Gen.
viii. 22

24 Hów is the cóld^a distríbuted,
     Or the stórm-blast scáttered on eárth ?

^b Cf. Ps.
lxv. 9

25 Who ópened^b the chánnel of clóud-burst,
     And the wáy for the flásh of the thúnder,
26 Causing ráin on lánd without mán,
     On úninhábited wílderness,

^c Cf. Ps.
lxv. 12

27 Sóaking the désolate wáste^c
     Till it spríng with gérms of gráss ?

The mystery of the rain in its manifold forms
of dew and ice.

28 Háth the ráin a fáther ?
     Or whó hath begótten the déw-drops ?
29 The íce ? from whose wómb came it fórth ?
     The hóar-frost of héaven ? who géndered it ?
30 The wáters are hídden like stóne,
     And the fáce of the déep is congéaled.

v. 24. Instead of *Ôr, light,* I suggest *Qôr, cold,* as in Gen. viii. 22. The
Septuagint read *hoar-frost.*
vv. 26, 27. If God's mercies fall on the uninhabited wilderness He must
have purposes that reach beyond the world of man. If so, Job should wait.
v. 30. The waters are here pictured as "hiding themselves" because,
under the action of frost, they become still as stone. The whole passage is
closely parallel with Ps. cxlvii. 17, especially if we there adopt the emendation
proposed by Duhm, *By reason of His frost the waters stand still.*

The mystery of the stars.

31 Dost thou fásten the bánds of the Pleíades ?
   Or lóosen the fétters of Oríon ?
32 Dost thou bríng Mazzaróth in his séason ?
   Dost thou gúide the Béar with its sóns ?
33 Dost thou knów the státutes of héaven ?
   Didst thou fíx their domínion in eárth ?

Who is it that ordereth the clouds and lightnings
to a beneficent end ?

34 Dost thou ráise thy vóice to the clóud,
   So that wáters abúndant obéy^a them ?   ª See
Sept.
35 Dost thou spéed on their érrand the líghtnings,
   That they ánswer thee, "Hére we áre" ?
36 Whó hath put wísdom withín them (?)
   Or impárted a míndlike intélligence ?
37 Who coúnteth (?) the skíes by wísdom ?
   Who dráineth the bóttles of héaven,
38 When the dúst runs fírm in a máss,
   And the clóds cleave fást togéther ?

vv. 31-33. The four constellations here named point to the four seasons of the year. The Covenant of Creation implies the fixed order of the Seasons, "cold and heat, summer and winter" (Gen. ix. 22). This Covenant is ordained by God and has meanings full of promise, beyond man's thought.
   "The stars still write their golden purposes
       On heaven's high palimpsest, and no man sees."
                                               (Francis Thompson.)
   v. 36. The translation of this difficult verse is merely provisional. The *wisdom* and *intelligence* refer, I think, not to the mind of man but to the storms and clouds and lightnings, which God has made thus to respond to His thought and to hearken to the voice of His words.
   v. 37. The word *counteth* seems here out of place: but by changing one letter we might read *garnisheth* as in chap. xxvi. 13. See Kittel's text.

*The thought now turns to the animal world. Who is it that takes
thought for the lions and ravens? Ought not man, then, to
trust ?*

39 Dost thóu hunt the préy for the lióness,
    And appéase the desíre of the yóung-lions ᵃ,
40 What tíme they cóuch in their déns,
    And stáy lying wáit in the cóvert ?

ᵇ Cf. Ps.
cxlvii. 9

41 Who provídeth the ráven ᵇ its fóod,
    When his yóung ones crý unto Gód ?

ᶜ Gloss

                [They stray lacking meat.] ᶜ

39 1 Didst thou fíx the tímes of the róck-goats ?
       Or appóint when the hínds should cálve ?
    2 Dost thou número the mónths they fulfíl ?
       Or fíx the tíme they bring fórth ?
    3 They bów down and bríng forth their yóung,
       Their paíns they cast óff and recóver.

ᵈ *open field*

    4 Their yóung ones grow úp in the ópen ᵈ,
       They go fórth and retúrn not agáin.

The joy of God in the freedom of wild life.

    5 Who sént the wild-áss into fréedom ?
       Who lóosed the bánds of the kúlan ᵉ,

ᵉ Another
name for
the wild-
ass

    6 Whose hóme I have máde the wílderness,
       And whose dwélling (I máde) the salt mársh ?
    7 He scórns the cíty dín :
       He héars no shóut of the táskmaster.
    8 His pásture the ránge of the moúntains,
       And his quést each thíng that is gréen.

    v. 3ᵇ. This line is too short for the metre while *v.* 4ᵃ is too long in the
Hebrew text. I therefore suggest reading the first word of *v.* 4ᵃ with *v.* 3ᵇ.
The sense of *recover* is found in Is. xxxviii. 16.

9 Will the óryx be wílling to sérve thee ?
   Or wíll he abíde by thy críb ?
10 Wilt thou bínd his yóke with a thóng^a ?
   Will he hárrow the válleys behínd thee ?
11 Wilt thou trúst to his gréatness of stréngth,
   And léave unto hím thy lábours ?
12 Wilt thou trúst him to bríng home thy séed,
   And to gárner (the córn of) thy thréshing-floor ?

ᵃ See
Sept.

*The ostrich.   Its so-called " folly" is a Divine arrangement
for its safety.*

13 Though the óstrich's wíng be shówy,
   Is it pínion for bróoding or flíght ?
14 Nay, she léaveth her éggs to the eárth,
   And kéepeth them wárm in the dúst,
15 And forgétteth that fóot may crúsh them,
   Or béast of the fiéld may tréad them.
16 She is hárd to her yoúng as not hérs ;
   Unconcérned, though her lábour be váin.
17 For Gód made her lácking in wísdom,
   Not impárting to hér understánding.
18 What tíme she bestírs her for flíght,
   She can móck at the hórse and his ríder.

The horse.

19 Dost thou gíve to the hórse his stréngth ?
   Dost thou clóthe his néck as with thúnder ?

vv. 10–12. The picture of the fierce wild-ox dragging the harrow behind
his master and left untended as a quiet beast of burden is very effective.

v. 13ᵇ. Literally *Is it a pinion kindly* (i.e. like that of the *stork* whose name
denotes its *kindly* care of its young) *and feathered* (i.e. like that of the eagle,
Ezek. xvii. 7, for flight). The ostrich is not fitted for either of these purposes,
but God, in compensation for the former, deprives her of the motherly
instinct (*vv.* 14–17) ; and in compensation for the latter, gives her a swiftness
on foot which can set the horse at defiance (*v.* 18).

20 Dost thou gíve him the crásh of the lócust ?
   That glóry and térror of nóstril[a] !
21 He páweth the válley and exúlteth ;
   In stréngth he goes fórth to meet wéapons.
22 He mócketh at féar, undismáyed ;
   Nor túrneth he báck from the swórd.
23 Agáinst him the quíver may ríng,
   The fláme of the spéar and the jávelin.
24 He devóurs the gróund with fierce ónset,
   And he cánnot stand stíll at the trúmpet.
25 At the trúmpet he saíth, " Ahá ! "
   For he scénteth the báttle from afár,
   The thúnder of cáptains, and shóuting.

vv. 19 ff. Dryden has paraphrased this description of the war-horse some-
what feebly as follows :
   " The fiery courser, when he hears from far
   The sprightly trumpets and the shouts of war,
   Pricks up his ears, and trembling with delight,
   Shifts place, and paws, and hopes the promised fight ;
   On his right shoulder his thick mane reclined,
   Ruffles at speed, and dances in the wind.
   Eager he stands,—then, starting with a bound,
   He turns the turf, and shakes the solid ground ;
   Fire from his eyes, clouds from his nostrils flow,
   He bears his rider headlong on the foe."

v. 20[a]. If the text be correct it must refer to the sound of the rushing
locust-swarm. In Rev. ix. 7 ff. the locusts are compared to war-horses in full
panoply, "And they had breastplates, as it were breastplates of iron ; and
the sound of their wings was as the sound of chariots, *and of many horses
rushing to war*" (R.V.).

v. 21. In the Hebrew text the first line is too long and the second too
short for the metre : but all becomes clear if we divide the verse as I have
done in my translation.

v. 24[b]. The text might literally be translated, *And he cannot stand still at
the voice of trumpet.* But the words *at the voice* have, I think, been added as a
gloss. Certainly the metre is better without them.

v. 25. *At the trumpet*, lit. *In the abundance of the trumpet*, or, as we should say,
In the thick of the trumpets.

Who taught the hawk tribe the instinct whereby they find their
way in the air, either for migration or for food?

26 Doth the háwk soar alóft through thý wisdom,
　　And spréad out his wíngs to the sóuth?
27 Doth the gríffon mount úp at thý telling?
　　Or the vúlture make nést on hígh?
28 He dwélls and hómes on the crág,
　　On the tóoth of the crág and fórtress.
29 From thénce he spíes his fóod,
　　And his éyes behóld it afár.
30 His yoúng ones súck up blóod;
　　And whére the slain áre—there is hé[a].

Lk. xvii.
37

vv. 26 ff.　Pope has expressed the same thought:
　　"Who taught the nations of the field and wood
　　To shun their poison and to choose their food?

　　.　.　.　.　.　.　.　.　.　.

　　Who bid the stork, Columbus-like, explore
　　Heavens not his own, and worlds unknown before?
　　Who calls the councils, states the certain day,
　　Who forms the phalanx, and who points the way?
　　God, in the nature of each being, founds
　　Its proper bliss, and sets its proper bounds:
　　But as He framed a whole, the whole to bless,
　　On mutual wants built mutual happiness:
　　So from the first, eternal order ran,
　　And creature link'd to creature, man to man."

v. 27.　The *nesher* is not the *eagle* but the "Griffon-Vulture." "A majestic bird, most abundant and never out of sight, whether on the mountains or the plains of Palestine. Everywhere it is a feature in the sky, as it circles higher and higher, till lost to all but the keenest sight, and then rapidly swoops down again." See Driver on Deut. xiv. 12.

Instead of the word כִּי (*v.* 27ᵇ), which makes no sense, I suggest דִיָּה, *the vulture*, which is coupled with *nesher* in Deut. xiv. 12 f.

40 1 And Jahveh answered Job and said:

If Job thinks he can improve upon the ordering of the world,
let him explain his method.

2 Will the cénsurer stríve with Shaddáï ?
Let Gód's instrúctor ánswer it.

3 And Job answered Jahveh and said:

Job begins to recognise the Divine purpose which
lies behind the power.

4 I am méan and whát can I ánswer Thee ?
I láy mine hánd on my móuth.
5 I have spóken ónce, but repéat not ;
Yea twíce, but néver agáin.

6 Then Jahveh answered Job out of the whirlwind and
said :

If Job thinks it such an easy thing to root out all wickedness from
the world, let him put himself in God's place.

7 Gírd now thy lóins like a mán ;
I will ásk thee ; infórm Me, I práy.
8 Wilt thóu disallów My ríght ?
Condemn Mé, that thóu mayest seem júst ?
9 Hast thóu an árm like Gód ?
And with vóice like Hís canst thou thúnder ?
10 Then déck thee with príde and májesty ;
Arráy thee with glóry and spléndour.
11 Pour róund thee thy fúry of ánger :
^a *each*   Behóld and lay lów all príde^a.
proud one
12 Behóld each próud one and húmble him ;
And crúsh the wícked instánter.

vv. 6, 7. These verses are a repetition of chap. xxxviii. 1, 3 and I suspect
that they are here out of place.

13 Híde them in dúst altogéther ;
   Bínd in the príson^a their fáces.

14 Then Í will conféss of thée
   That thine ówn right hánd can sáve thee.

*Let Job consider that there are other creatures that share
God's care with man, e.g. Behemoth.*

15 Behóld the great-béasts (made) with thée—
   He éateth gráss like the óx.
16 Behóld now his stréngth in his lóins ;
   And his fórce in the múscles of his bélly.
17 He móveth his táil like a cédar ;
   And the sínews of his thíghs (?) are close-knít.
18 His bónes are like túbes of brónze ;
   His ríbs like bárs of íron.
19 The fírst of God's wáys is hé ;
   He is máde the lórd of his féllows.
20 The moúntains yiéld him their frúits ;
   Where the béasts of the fiéld all pláy.

v. 13ᵇ. The reference is, I think, to the fact that when a man was condemned his face was covered (Esth. vii. 8).

v. 15. The text has "Behold now the great beasts (*behemoth*) which I made
with thee." But the line is too long for the metre and the Septuagint rightly
omits the words, *which I made*. I regard these words as a gloss, but they
express the right meaning.

On the sixth "day" of Creation God made the *great-beasts* and also *man*.
Job is reminded of the fact that God's care extends to other creatures which
are, in some respects, superior to man.

v. 19. The word *first* or *beginning* is used of a firstborn son (e.g. Gen. xlix.
3). The second member of the verse is extremely difficult, but if we emend
the text, as suggested in Kittel's Hebrew Bible we may render, *He is made the
taskmaster of his fellows*, i.e. like a firstborn son he is lord over his brethren.
Thus the parallelism is preserved.

v. 20. In spite of his great strength he feeds upon grass, and the wild life
of the fields is safe around him.

21 In the lótus-sháde he lies dówn,
   In the cóvert of réed and fén.
22 The lótus trees yiéld him their shélter ;
   The wíllows of the bróok their sháde.
23 Though a ríver should ráge he féars not ;
   He is cálm though a Jórdan swéll.
24 Through his éyes can one táke him in snáres ?
   Can one piérce through his nóse to his móuth ?

Leviathan or the crocodile.

^a *Levia-*
than

41 1 Canst thou dráw out the Mónster^a with hóok ?
      Or bínd his tóngue with a córd ?

^b *I.e. of*
rushes

2 Canst thou pút a wísp^b through his gílls ?
  Or piérce his jáw with a thórn ?
3 Will he máke to thee gréat supplicátions ?
  Will he spéak to thee ténder-entréaty ?
4 Will he énter with thée into cóvenant,
  To táke him as sérvant for éver ?
5 Wilt thou pláy with hím as with bírd,

^c Lit. *bind*

  And cáge^c him úp for thy máidens ?
6 Shall the cómpanies féast upón him,
  And divíde him úp for the mérchants ?
7 Canst thou fíll his bódy with bárbs,
  And his héad with the físh-harpóon ?

vv. 23, 24. These verses are wrongly divided in the text.

   The words, *to his mouth*, which, in the text, come at the end of *v.* 23^b and
make that line too long for the metre, should, I think, be read at the end of
v. 24^b ; and that verse should be divided differently. The general sense is
" Can you catch this monster of the rivers as you would a little fish ? "

   vv. 1, 2. Here we have a picture of catching a fish and carrying it home,
strung on a rush or hooked on a thorn.

   v. 4. *Servant for ever.* A slave so contented that he refuses the offer of
his freedom. See Exod. xxi. 6 ; Deut. xv. 17.

   v. 6. *Feast.* The word is used for *making great provision* (2 Kings vi. 23).
But it may also have the sense of *make traffic.* It is God, not man, who gives
Leviathan to be *food for the desert folk* (Ps. lxxiv. 14).

8 Lay (ónce) thine hánd upón him :
Remémber the fíght !—Not agáin !
9 Behóld his hópe is proved fálse !
At the mére sight of hím he's cast dówn.
10 None so crúel to sélf as to roúse him.
Who is hé that can stánd befóre him ?
11 Who éver faced hím and was sáfe[a] ?
Benéath the whole héaven not óne !
12 I wíll not be sílent respécting[b] him
.   .   .   .[c]
13 Who can ópen the frónt of his gárment ?
Who can énter his doúble mail-cóat[b] ?
14 Who unfólded the dóors of his fáce ?
There is térror aroúnd his téeth.
15 His báck[b] is chánnels of shiélds ;
Shut úp all roúnd as a séal ;
16 So néar the óne to the óther,
That aír cannot páss betwéen.
17 They cléave éach to his féllow ;
They hold fást and cánnot be súndered.
18 His néesings flásh forth líght ;
His éyes are like éyelids of dáwn.
19 Flaming tórches go oút from his moúth ;
Spárklets of fíre fly oút.
20 Smóke goes fórth from his nóstrils,
Like a séething pót and rush-fíre.
21 His gréed[d] would kíndle cóals ;
And a fláme goes fórth from his moúth.
22 On his néck there dwélleth stréngth ;
And destrúction rúnneth befóre him[b].

[a] See Sept.

[b] Sept.
[c] Text corrupt

[d] *appetite*

vv. 10, 11. I have followed the emendations of the text suggested in Kittel's edition, for, as Dr Driver remarks, "a reference to God hardly seems in place here." The difference between the affix for *him* and the affix for *me* is, in the Hebrew, very slight.

23 The flákes (?) of his flésh are close-knít,
     Fírm upón him, immóveable.
24 His héart is fírm as stóne ;
     As néther-míllstone fírm.
25 When he ríses the stróng-ones do féar,
     At the bréakers, are strícken with pánic.
26 No swórd can stánd to appróach him,
     Or spéar or dárt or sháft.
27 He coúnteth íron as stráw,
     And bráss as rótten wóod.
28 No árrow can pút him to flíght ;
     Slíng-stones on hím are turned cháff.
29 Clúbs are coúnted as réed[a] ;
     And he mócks at the whíz of the jávelin.
30 His láir[a] is the shárp rock-shérds ;
     He coúcheth his lóins on the múd.
31 He can máke the Deep bóil like a pót ;
     He can stír the Séa like an óintment.
32 There shíneth a páth in his wáke ;
     One might thínk the Déep to be hóary.
33 There ís not his líke upon eárth ;
     A créature that's máde without dréad.
34 But hím each hígh one féars,
     He is kíng over áll the próudest.

[a] Sept.

v. 25. The swirl of the crocodile in its rush through the water is here pictured.

v. 30. *His loins.* The word has this meaning in the Hebrew of the Targum (e.g. on chap. xl. 16, *his strength is in his loins*) and in Dan. v. 6. The crocodile is quite at home among the sharpest pointed rocks and he lies, half buried in the mud banks, waiting for his prey.

v. 32. The Deep (*Tehôm*) is personified like *Tiamat* in the Babylonian mythology.

v. 34. The metre requires this slight alteration of the text which is, on other grounds, suggested in Kittel's critical notes. *All the proudest,* lit. *all the sons of pride,* cf. chap. xxviii. 8. But the Sept. and other Versions read *All (that move) in the waters* (cf. Gen. i. 20).

42 1 And Job answered Jahveh and said:

2 I knów that Thóu canst do áll things,
   That no púrpose of Thíne is restráined :
   Thérefore I úttered, not grásping,
   Thíngs far beyónd me, past knówing !

vv. 2–6.   In the Hebrew text *Who is this that hideth counsel without knowledge ?*
has been introduced from xxxviii. 2 and *Hear now, and I will speak ; I will ask
thee ; inform Me, I pray* from xxxviii. 3 ; xl. 7.   These insertions spoil the
poetry and the sense, I have therefore omitted them.

   Therefore I uttered.   Job does not here merely refer to hasty speech that
he has used about God, but rather to the whole outcome of his thoughts about
those purposes of God which he now sees to have been "too wonderful for
him."   The best comment is Ps. xl. 5, *Thy marvels and Thy purposes to us-ward !...
Would I tell them and speak of them ; they outnumber all recounting.*

   It is important again to note that though the Divine speeches contain
nothing new to Job, regarding the *power* of God, yet they do suggest to him a
wholly new thought as to a Divine *purpose* in Creation.   This it is that makes
all the difference in life.

> " All things then
> Would minister to joy ; then should thine heart
> Be heal'd and harmonised, and thou would'st feel
> God, always, everywhere, and all in all."
>
> (Southey.)

From an artistic point of view the Poem should end here : but the Writer
who, in the Prologue, had taken the reader, as it were, behind the scenes,
now seeks to justify the ways of God with Israel by picturing the restored
happiness of the Suffering Servant.   Israel, after the Captivity, was to receive
the double of good (Is. lxi. 7 ; Zech. ix. 12).   It was therefore necessary that
Job should receive *the double* (xlii. 10).   This is carried out in detail as to his
possessions : his *seven thousand sheep* (i. 3) become *fourteen thousand* (xlii. 12) ;
his *three thousand camels* become *six thousand* : his *five hundred yoke of oxen* and
his *five hundred she-asses* become, in each case, *a thousand.*

   But, more than this, Job is now recognised by God as *My Servant* (xlii. 7 :
cf. i. 8 ; ii. 3).   As such he makes intercession for the transgressors (*v.* 9).
Probably the Second Isaiah is later than the Book of Job.   Certainly the
work of the Suffering Servant is there more fully developed : but, in Job, we
find the same germs of thought.

5 By mérest héarsay I héard Thee,
   But nów mine éye hath séen Thee.
6 Thérefore it ís I lóathe (me),
   And repént in dúst and áshes.

THE EPILOGUE

God justifies Job, His Suffering Servant, before his friends and he makes intercession for their trans-gressions.

7   And it came to pass, after Jahveh had spoken these words unto Job, that Jahveh said unto Eliphaz the Temanite, Mine anger is kindled against thee and against thy two friends : for ye have not spoken of Me the thing that is right, as My servant Job hath.

8   And now take you seven bullocks and seven rams and go to My Servant Job that ye may offer for yourselves a burnt offering ; and My Servant Job shall pray for you, for him will I accept, so that I may not award folly unto you, for that ye have not spoken of Me the thing that is right, as My Servant Job hath.

9   So they went, Eliphaz the Temanite and Bildad the Shuhite and Zophar the Naamathite, and they did as Jahveh commanded them : and Jahveh accepted Job.

Because the Suffering Servant intercedes for transgressors
God gives him a restored life, a double for all he has
endured (cf. Is. xl. 2).

10 And Jahveh turned the captivity of Job on his praying
for his friends : and Jahveh added the double to all that
Job had had.

11 And there came unto him all his brethren, and all his
sisters, and all his former friends, and they did eat bread
with him in his house : and they condoled with him and
comforted him concerning all the evil that Jahveh had
brought upon him : and they gave him each one a
kesitah, and each one a ring of gold.

12 And Jahveh blessed the latter end of Job more than his
beginning ; and he had fourteen thousand sheep, and six
thousand camels, and a thousand yoke of oxen, and a
thousand she-asses.

13 And he had seven sons and three daughters.

14 And he called the name of the one Jemimah, and the
name of the second Keziah, and the name of the third
Keren-happūch.

15 And there were not found women, so beautiful as the
daughters of Job, in all the land : and their father gave
them inheritance among their brethren.

16 And Job lived, after this, a hundred and forty years,
and saw his sons and his sons' sons, even four genera-
tions.

17 So Job died, old and full of days.

APPENDIX

THE ELIHU SPEECHES

It is now generally recognised that the Elihu speeches had no place in the original poem but that they were introduced by a later writer who, probably on the grounds of reverence, objected to the intervention of God as a Speaker. With this end in view he introduces *Elihu*, whose name is akin to *Elijah*, to speak on behalf of God. Elihu is full of indignation against the three "friends" because they had failed to vindicate God against Job (xxxii. 3, 13, 15 f.), but he is equally indignant against Job because his language has been wanting in reverence towards God (xxxiii. 1–12 : xxxiv. 5 ff., 35–37 : xxxv. 16). Elihu is fully convinced that he has a new and important contribution to make to the argument ; but it is impossible to acquit him of conceit (xxxii. 7 ff., 14, 15–20).

His actual contribution to the argument amounts to this, that he develops more fully the remedial motive of God's judgements (xxxiii. 14–28 : xxxvi. 8 ff.). He also has much to say on the vastness of God's plan in creation as necessarily exceeding the grasp of human intellect. Here he borrows much from those Divine speeches to which he objected (xxxvi. 26–xxxvii. 24).

The style of the Elihu passages is turgid and the text in many places corrupt. There are, however, some passages of real beauty.

In conclusion we may say that if Elihu had been known to the Author of xlii. 7 he would certainly have been included in the condemnation passed upon the three "friends."

3   1 So these three men ceased from answering Job, because
he was righteous in his own eyes.
2 Then was kindled the anger of Elihu the son of Barachel
the Buzite, of the family of Ram : against Job was his anger
kindled, because he justified himself rather than God.
3 And against his three friends was his anger kindled, because
they had found no answer, and had condemned Job.
4 Now Elihu had waited to address Job, because they were
elder than he.
5 And when Elihu saw that there was no answer in the mouth
of these three men, then his wrath was kindled.
6 And Elihu the son of Barachel the Buzite answered and
said :

Elihu speaks with the confidence of youth.

I ám but yóung in dáys,
And yé are véry óld ;
Só I held báck, and I féared
To expréss to yóu my opínion.
7 I thóught that dáys should spéak,
Long yéars should téach (men) wísdom.
8 But 'tís the spírit in mán ;
And the bréath of Shaddái makes them wíse.
9 It ís not the gréat that are wíse ;
Nor the áged that cómprehend júdgement.
10 Thérefore say Í, " Hear mé ;
I álso will shéw mine opínion."

He is fully convinced that his seniors are all wrong.

11 Behóld, I awáited your wórds ;
I lént mine éar to your réasons,
While yé sought oút your wórds,
And Í unto yóu gave atténtion.

12 Lo, nóne convícted Jób,
    Not óne of you ánswered his wórds.

He protests against the necessity of the Divine speeches. He feels
that he himself is quite competent to answer Job.

13 Nor sáy ye, "Wé have found wísdom,
    Gód, not mán, shall abáse him."
14 He addréssed himself nót unto mé,
    Else I'd ánswered him nót with your wórds.

Elihu breaks off into a soliloquy.

15 Dumbfóunded, they ánswer no móre !
    Their phráses have áll desérted them !
16 Shall I wáit then becaúse they speak nót,
    Becaúse they stand stíll and replý not ?
17 I tóo will ánswer for mý part ;
    I tóo will shéw mine opínion.
18 For fúll of wórds am Í ;
    The spírit withín me constráineth.
19 I ám as wíne unvénted,
    As wíne-skins réady to búrst.
20 I must spéak to gét me relíef ;
    Must ópen my líps and make ánswer.

Elihu has but a short time on earth and
cannot afford to flatter.

21 May I néver regárd man's pérson ;
    Or bestów upon mán my títles[a].

 ᵃ *flattery*

vv. 13 f.   If the text be correct it would seem to mean, " Do not congratulate
yourselves on the thought that God will humble Job. There is no need for
God to intervene. I am quite capable of meeting all his arguments." " The
verse is a direct polemic against the poet, a strong assertion that the Divine
speeches which follow had been better omitted." (Peake.)

22 For I knów not hów to give títles ;
   Sóon my Máker must táke me.

*Elihu will shew Job that he is wrong ; not, as the friends assert,
in proclaiming his innocence, but in regarding God as his
enemy.*

33 1 Héar now my spéech, O Jób ;
   And to áll my wórds give éar.
   2 Behóld, I have ópened my móuth ;
   My tóngue in my pálate hath spóken.
   3 My héart doth indíte words of knówledge ;
   My líps do spéak sincérely.
   4 The Spírit of Gód hath máde me ;
   And the bréath of Shaddáï gives me lífe.
   5 Ánswer me thís if thou cánst ;
   Set in órder ᵃ befóre me ; stand úp.   ᵃ I.e.
                                                      arguments

*I heard you (ix. 32–35 : xiii. 20–22) request that God might lay
His power down and meet you like a man. Here now stand I
for God. A man like yourself.*

   6 Here am Í, for Gód, at thy wórd :
   I tóo am frámed of cláy.
   7 Lo, no térror of míne need affríght thee ;
   Nor mine hánd ᵇ weigh héavy upón thee.   ᵇ Sept.

*Elihu reminds Job of what he had heard him say respecting God's
hostility. (See ix. 21 : x. 7 : xiii. 27 : xiv. 16 : xvi. 17 :
xxvii. 2–6.)*

   8 Náy, thou didst sáy in mine éars,
   And I héard the soúnd of thy wórds,

v. 22. The verse is difficult. The Vulgate had a different text.
   v. 3. The slight alteration suggested in Kittel's text is absolutely required
by the metre.

9 "I am cléan (and) withoút transgréssion ;
   Spótless am Í, without gúilt :
10 Ló, He finds prétexts agáinst me,
   He regárdeth mé as His énemy[a] ;
11 He pútteth my féet in the stócks[b],
   He márketh áll my páths."
12 Lo, in thís thou art fár from júst ;
   For Gód is gréat beyond mán.

[a] xiii. 24:
xix. 11:
xxx. 21
[b] xiii. 27

*Why should Job complain that God does not answer him in words ?
As a matter of fact God does speak in many ways, if men
would but attend to the warnings.*

13 Whý hast thou pléaded agáinst Him,
   That, "He ánswereth nót my wórds" ?
14 Nay—óne way spéaketh Gód,
   And in twó, though nóne percéiveth :
15 In a dréam, in a vísion of níght,
   [When déep-sleep fálls on mén,][c]
   In slúmberings ón the béd :
16 Thén He unvéils men's éar,
   And púts them in dréad[d] with térrors ;

[c] iv. 13
[d] Sept.

v. 12[a]. The text adds *I will answer thee* but this makes the line too long for the metre and is evidently a gloss. The Septuagint had quite a different text.

Elihu does not mean that because God is great He can do no wrong, but rather that His ends and purposes are beyond the power of mortal men to trace, and that therefore affliction does not imply His hostility as Job supposes. Still his argument is not convincing.

v. 13[b]. We read *my words* instead of *His words*. See Duhm and Kittel's text. Job has again and again complained that God will not answer him.

v. 15[b]. This line is not needed. It has evidently been copied from chap. iv. 13 where it occurs in a similar context.

17 To túrn man asíde from his dóings :
   So He hídeth príde from mán.
18 He would kéep back his sóul from the pít,
   And his lífe from pássing by wéapon.

*Another way in which God warns is by sickness. The writer evi-
dently has Ps. cvii. 17–22 in mind. (Cf. Chap. xxxvi. 8–11.)
The influence of this Psalm should be noted also in Chap. xii.
21–25.*

19 Or He smítes^a him with páin on his béd,
   Uncéasing strífe in his bónes.
20 So his lífe abhórreth fóod^b,
   And his sóul the chóicest dáinties.
21 So his flésh is wásted to léanness,
   And his bónes with emáciátion.
22 So his sóul draweth nígh to the pít,
   And his lífe to the ángels of déath.

^a Sept.
Vulg. Syr.

^b Cf. Ps.
cvii. 18

*But God is really waiting for the Recording Angel to find some
trace of penitence that He may shew mercy.*

23 If there bé, on hís part, an ángel,
   [An ádvocate, óne in a thóusand,]^c
   To téll, of that mán, his upríghtness.
24 Thén He shews píty and sáith,
   "Redéem him from góing to the pít,
   [I have found a ransom—]^c "

^c ? Gloss

v. 17^b. The text is uncertain.
v. 21. My translation is based on an emendation of the text which I
proposed in a note on the text of Job in the *J. T. S.* (October 1913).
v. 24^c. This line is too short for the metre. As in other cases where we
have three lines in the verse it is, almost certainly, a gloss.
   There is a saying in the *Pirqe Aboth* (iv. 15), " He who performs one
precept has gotten to himself one advocate (paraclete)," on which Taylor
quotes *Shemoth Rabbah* xxxii : " If a man performs one precept, the Holy One,
blessed is He, gives him one angel to guard him."

25 Then his flésh becomes frésher than chíldhood,
   He retúrns to the dáys of his yóuth :
26 He práyeth to Gód with accéptance ;
   So he séeth His fáce with júbile[a].

[The passage which follows is in prose.]

So He restoreth unto man his righteousness.   27 He singeth (?) before men, and saith, "I have sinned, and perverted that which was right and it was not requited unto me : 28 He hath redeemed my soul from going into the pit, and my life shall behold the light."

Such is the gracious purpose of affliction.

29 All thís, behóld, God dóeth,
   Twíce, yea thríce, with mán ;
30 To bríng back his sóul from the pít,
   To be líghted with líght of lífe.
31 Mark wéll, O Jób, hear mé ;
   Be sílent and I will spéak.
32 If there ís a respónse, give ánswer ;
   Spéak, for I wísh thy acquíttal.
33 If nót, then do thóu hear mé ;
   Be stíll while I téach thee wísdom.

34 1 And Elihu answered and said :

Elihu appeals to all who have wisdom to judge the truth of his contention.

2 Héarken, ye wíse, to my wórds ;
   Give éar to me, yé that have knówledge.

v. 32. The emphasis on the word *is* implies that Elihu does not see how Job can have any answer to his argument.   Men like Elihu feel this comfortable confidence.

3 "For the éar makes tést of wórds,
   As the pálate tásteth by éating^a."   ^a xii. 11
4 Let us fínd out thát which is ríght :
   Let us knów, by oursélves, what is góod.

Iob claimed that God has treated him unfairly (cf. xxxiii. 9–11).

5 For Jób did sáy, "I have ríght,
   And Gód hath pervérted my caúse :
6 In the mátter of júdgement I'm wrónged :
   Déadly my wóund, though innócent."

To make such a charge against God is blasphemy.

7 Was there éver a mán like Jób,
   That dránk in scóffing like wáter^b ?   ^b xv. 16
8 That wént in the rúck of ill-dóers^c,   ^c xxii. 15
   Wálking with wícked mén ?
9 For he saíth, "No prófit hath mán
   In táking delíght in Gód."

Man's conception of justice comes from God : it is therefore im-
possible that God Himself should be unjust.   A " diffuse
restatement of Bildad's maxim, viii. 3 " (Peake).

10 Héar me, ye mén of understánding,
   Forbíd it that Gód should be wícked !
   Or that Shaddáï should do wróng !
11 For He páys to éach his wórk,
   And requítes him áfter his wáy.
12 Nay, trúly, God cánnot do wróng,
   Nor Shaddáï be pervérter of jústice !
13 Who entrústed Hím with His eárth ?
   Or sét Him óver the Úniverse ?

vv. 7–9.   Elihu exaggerates his case.   But see chaps. ix. 22 ; xxi. 7 ff.   In
these verses Elihu does but repeat in stronger language the thoughts of
Eliphaz.

14 If He táke to Himsélf His Spírit^a,
   And withdráw His bréath to Himsélf,
15 All flésh at ónce would expíre^b,
   And mán would retúrn unto dúst^b.

Elihu now appeals to Job.

16 If thou hást understánding, hear thís ;
   Give éar to the voíce of my wórds.
17 Could a háter of jústice be rúler ?
   Or woúldst thou condémn the All-júst ?
18 Should one sáy of a kíng, " Good-for-nóthing " ?
   Or applý the term " Wícked " to nóbles ?

How much more then is respect due to the King of kings ?

19 Then of Hím that respécteth not prínces !
   That regárdeth not rích more than póor !
c ? Gloss   [For they áll are the wórk of His hánds.]^c

[*The verse which follows seems also to be the work of a later prose
writer, with a possible reference to the destruction of Senna-
cherib's host.*]

20 In a moment they die and at midnight the people are
   overthrown and perish, and the mighty are removed not by
   (any human) hand.

21 His éyes are upón man's wáys,
   And áll his stéps He séeth.
22 No dárkness, no déath-shade exísts,
   Where wórkers of wróng may be hídden.
d Text   23 For there ís, for mán, no appóintment^d
doubtful   To cóme into júdgement with Gód.

v. 17. Job might easily have answered, " It is just there where my
difficulty lies."

No inquisition can be set upon His actions.

24 He bréaketh the míghty unséarchably,
And othérs He séts in their pláce.

.   .   .   .   .   .ᵃ

26 They are crúshed as wícked mén,
He smítes them where áll can sée;
27 Becaúse that they swérved from fóllowing Him,
And discárded áll His wáys;
28 Bringing úpᵇ the crý of the póor,
So the gróan of the néedy He héars.

ᵃ Text
corrupt

ᵇ I.e. *to
God*

[*The four verses which follow are in prose, and the
text is very doubtful.*]

29 For He it is that gives quiet, and who can cause unrest ?   And
if He should hide His face, who can behold Him?   And
(this is so) whether in the case of a nation or an individual :
30 So that a godless man should not reign, (and that such)
should not be snares to a people.
31 For unto God he said, "I have borne (my iniquity), I will
not offend;
32 Only that which I see not do Thou teach me; if I have done
iniquity, I will do it no more."

Shall a man dictate to God?

33 Múst He reqúite in thý fashion,
That thóu hast refúsed (His corréction) ?
Then thóu must be chóoser, not Í,
And thát which thou knówest speak oút !

v. 25. The greater part of this verse is omitted (see Kittel's text). The
last word of the verse is read with *v.* 26ᵃ where, indeed, it is required by the
metre.

34 The thínking will sáy with mé ;
    And the wíse with mé will agrée
35 That Jób doth spéak without knówledge,
    And his wórds are withoút intélligence.
36 O that Jób might be próved to the úttermost,
    Becaúse of his ímpious ánswers !
37 Since he áddeth rebéllion to sín,
    And múltiplies wórds against Gód.

35 1 And Elihu answered and said :

2 Is it thís thou dost thínk to be ríght,
    That thou sáy'st, " I am júster than Gód" ?
3 For thou sáyest, " Whát shall it 'vántage thee ?
    What gáin I móre than by sínning ? "
4 Í, then, will gíve thee an ánswer,
    And thy féllows alóng with thée.

The sky that is so high above us is a parable of the un-
approachableness of the God who is higher.

5 Lóok at the héavens and sée,
    And regárd the ský high abóve thee.
6 How afféctest thou Hím if thou sínnest ?
    What canst dó with thy mány transgréssions ?
7 Or if júst, what gívest thou Hím[a] ?
    Or whát doth He táke at thy hánd ?
8 For a mán like thysélf is thy wíckedness,
    For a són of mán thy ríghteousness.

[a] Cf. xxii. 2 f.

v. 3.   He means to say, " What gain is there in leading a good life more than in leading a life of sin ? "   Cf. chap. ix. 22.
vv. 6 ff.   Tennyson has expressed the same thought :
    " Forgive what seem'd my sin in me ;
        What seem'd my worth since I began ;
        For merit lives from man to man,
        And not from man, O Lord, to thee."

Elihu now turns to Job's complaint (Chap. xxiv.) that the cry of the
oppressed is unheeded by God. Elihu argues that this cry was
not really a prayer.

9 Through abúndant oppréssions men gróan ;
  Through the pówer of týrants they crý.
10 Yet nóne sayeth, "Whére is Gód^a,   ^a Gloss,
  The Gíver of Sóngs in the níght ;   *my Maker*
11 Who téacheth us móre than the béasts,
  Gives us wísdom beyónd the fówls ? "
12 They crý there—but Hé answers nót—
  Becaúse of the príde of ill-dóers.
13 Mere vánity Gód cannot héar ;
  Nor cán Shaddáí regárd it.

[*The next two verses are corrupt, giving neither sense nor metre ; we*
therefore omit them. They probably imply, "Still less can God
hear Job when, instead of waiting patiently, he complains that
he cannot see Him."]

16 Job ópens his móuth then váinly,
  And píles up wórds without knówledge.

36 1 Elihu also proceeded, and said :

Job is wrong in maintaining (cf. xxii. 12–15) that God does
not take note of what is done on earth.

2 Permít me a whíle, I will shéw thee ;
  For wórds still remáin for Gód.

vv. 9–13. God has given to man a gift denied to the beasts of the earth
and the fowls of the heaven, the gift of articulate prayer. If then He send
affliction, for some good end, and man merely cry like a beast in pain, how
can God "answer" his cry, since the whole object for which the affliction
was sent remains as before ? The reader will remember that Elihu is an
intense believer in the remedial motive of affliction : he must therefore
account for cases in which the remedy seems to fail.

3 I will fétch my knówledge from fár ;
   Will ascríbe the ríght to my Máker.
4 For trúly my wórds are no líe,
   One pérfect in knówledge is wíth thee.

Once more Elihu returns to the thought of Ps. cvii.

5 Behóld, God doth nót act with scórn ;
   He is míghty in stréngth of héart.
6 He wíll not presérve the wícked ;
^a *the*   And He dóes give their ríght to the wrónged^a.
afflicted
^b *His eyes* 7 From the ríghteous He withdráws not appróval^b ;
   But (séats them), with kíngs, on a thróne.
^c ?Gloss   [Yea, seats them for ever, and they are exalted.]^c
8 Or íf they be boúnd in cháins,
   Táken in córds of afflíction,
9 Then He télls them their wórk they have dóne ;
   Their transgréssions whereín they dealt proúdly.
10 So He ópens their éar to instrúction,
   And commánds they should túrn from iníquity.
11 Íf they obéy and do sérvice,
   They fínish their dáys in prospérity,
^d Gloss   [And their years in pleasures.]^d
12 If nót they pérish by wéapons,
   They díe wholly lácking in knówledge.
13 So the gódless in héart cherish ánger,
   They crý not (to Hím) when He bínds them.

v. 4^b.   It is generally assumed that Elihu applies this term to himself, but it is possible that he means God, on whose behalf he claims to speak. The Septuagint had a different text which, though we cannot accept it as it stands, suggests that the original text may have read, *One is with thee who understands knowledge.*

v. 13.   They are like brute beasts ; their affliction, that had a Divine meaning, moves them, not to prayer, but to blind anger.

14 Their sóul must díe in yóuth ;
And their lífe, like the próstitutes', (énds).

But, on the other hand, God's suffering servants find in the
affliction a revelation.   (Cf. Is. l. 4 f.)   This is God's purpose
with Job.

15 The súfferer He sáves through his súffering ;
And unvéils his éar through oppréssion.
16 Thee tóo He would lúre through tróuble
To spáciousness únconfíned.
[And that which is set on thy table should be full
of fatness.]ᵃ   ᵃ Gloss

But you, Job, are missing this good purpose of affliction and are
regarding it like those godless men of whom I have spoken ; and
therefore, instead of becoming remedial, it becomes penal.

17 Thou art fílled with the wícked man's júdgement ;
So júdgement and jústice do hóld thee.
18 Bewáre lest entíced to scórningᵇ,   ᵇ Text
And lét not high ránsom misléad thee.   doubtful
19 He will réckon thy wéalth as wórthless ;
And áll the fórce of thy stréngth.

Let not Job think to end his troubles in the night of death.   Suicide,
of which Job has spoken (vii. 15), is a terrible sin.

20 Desíre not thóu that níght,
In which péoples pérish at ónce.

v. 16.   Elihu here well expresses a noble thought.

v. 18.   The Hebrew text gives neither sense nor metre.   The suggestions
in Kittel's text help us to some extent to restore it.   But our translation is only
provisional.

v. 19.   An exceedingly difficult verse.   The words we translate *worthless*
literally signify *not gold*, i.e. according to the Hebrew idiom, *the very reverse of*
gold.   The general sense of the passage seems to be that Job must not delude
himself by supposing that any ransom will avail with God.

21 Beware ;—incline nót to iníquity ;
   For 'tis thís thou preférredst to súffering.
22 Lo, Gód, in His stréngth, doeth lóftily :
   Whó is a téacher like Hím ?
23 Whó hath enjóined Him His wáy ?
   Who can sáy, "It is wróng Thou hast dóne" ?
24 Remémber His wórk to exált ;
   The théme which mén have súng.
25 Mankínd as a whóle look thereón ;
   Yea, mórtals · behóld it from fár.
26 Lo, gréat is Gód, beyond kén !
   The cóunt of His yéars, beyond séarch !

Instances of God's greatness in the world of nature.
Compare the Divine Speeches.

ᵃ Kittel's
text

27 For He dráweth up dróps from the Séaᵃ,
   They distíl in ráin from His míst :
28 With whích the skíes drop dówn,
   And póur upon mán in abúndance.
29 Whó can understánd the cloud-spréadings ?
   The thúnderings of His clóud-pavílion ?
30 Lo, He spréadeth upón it His líght ;
   And the tóps of the móuntains He cóversᵃ.

God uses the thunder and the rain both for judgement and for
blessing. Elihu wishes to imply that it rests with Job
whether God's dispensations with him result in judgement or
in blessing.

ᵇ I.e. *the*
clouds
(*v.* 29)

31 For by thémᵇ He doeth júdgement on Péoples ;
   By thém too gives fóod in abúndance.

32 He táketh the Líght in both hánds ;
  And gíveth it chárge to its márk.
33 His thúnder decláreth concérning Him,
  A kíndling of wráth against sín.

37 1 At thís my héart doth trémble ;
  And léapeth úp from its pláce.
 2 Hark, hárk His tumúltuous voíce !
  And the róar that goes fórth from His móuth !
 3 Benéath the whole héaven He guídes it ;
  And its líght[a] to the bórders of eárth.
 4 Behínd it there róareth the voíce[b] ;
  He thúnders with voíce majéstic.
  [And He stayeth them not when His voice is heard.][c]

  .   .   .   .

 6 He saíth to the snów, "Fall on eárth" ;
  With the clóud-burst and ráin of His míght.
 7 By théir means He séals up mankínd ;
  That áll men may knów His wórk.
 8 The béasts then withdráw into cóverts ;
  And abíde withín their déns.
 9 The whírlwind then cómes from its chámber ;
  And the cóld from oút of its stórehouse.

[a] Or, *lightnings*
[b] *thunder*
[c] Gloss

v. 32[a]. If the text be correct it would signify, *He covereth up both hands with the Light*, or possibly, *He covers up the Light in His two hands.* The *Light* may also denote the *lightnings* ; but here too the thought is either for judgement or for mercy. The *Light* for blessing, the *lightnings* for destruction ; both have their mark.

v. 33[b]. The vowel points are wrong. See Kittel's text.

v. 4[c]. This line is not in metre and is evidently a comment by some early scribe.

v. 5. This verse is omitted, being merely a variant of *v.* 4[b] and xxxvi. 26[a].

v. 7. The winter months in which men cannot labour in the fields give pause for thought on God.

v. 9[b]. A slight correction of the text (see Kittel), which is accepted also by Driver.

ᵃ Lit.
breadth

ᵇ Cf.
chap.
xxxviii.
24;
Ps. cxliv.
6
ᶜ I.e. *the
cloud*
ᵈ I.e.
correction

ᵉ *wonders*

10 By the bréath of Gód He gives íce ;
    And the fréedomᵃ of wáters is stráitened.
11 He búrdens the thíck-cloud with háil (?)
    (Then) scátters the clóud with His líghtᵇ.
12 And itᶜ túrns itself roúnd in His guídance,
    To dó of áll He commánds it,
    On the fáce of His hábited eárth,
13 Whéther as ródᵈ for His eárth,
    Or whéther He bríng it in mércy.

*Let Job consider the mercy that lies behind the cloud
before he judge rashly of God.*

14 Héarken to thís, O Jób :
    Stand stíll and consíder God's wórksᵉ.
15 Dost thou knów when God gíves them a chárge ?
    Or makes líght to shíne from His clóud ?
16 Dost thou knów how the clóuds are bálanced,
    The wórksᵉ of the Pérfect-in-Knówledge ?
17 Thóu, whose gárments are wárm
    When eárth is stílled by sirócco,

v. 11. The rapid transition from darkness to light in the hail-storm is thus expressed by Shelley in his poem on *The Cloud* :
    "I wield the flail of the lashing hail,
      And whiten the green plains under,
    And then again I dissolve it in rain,
      And laugh as I pass in thunder."
v. 12. The cloud may be dispersed but only to build itself up again in new forms for an unceasing activity of service. I think that the third line of the verse is a later addition.
v. 15. The context leads us to expect that the first line refers to works of judgement and the second to works of mercy ; as though he had said, " Can you trace God's purposes in Nature ? And, if not, can you be sure that what, in your own life, seems to be His judgement may not be a message of mercy ?"

18 Dost thóu weld the skíes with Hím,
   All fírm as a mólten mírror ?

Elihu does not assert, with Eliphaz (xxii. 11), that the darkening of Job's heaven is due to his sin. But Job must wait for God.

19 Téach us what of Hím we should sáy ;
   For wé are restráined by the dárkness.
20 Shóuld it be sáid He's destróyed ?
   Should one thínk that He's swállowed úp ?
21 Yea, nów, though men sée not the líght,

v. 18. The Hebrew word for *firmament* signifies that which is *beaten out firm.*

vv. 19–21. My translation of these very difficult verses is founded upon some emendations of the text which I suggested in the *J. T. S.* (October 1913).

Elihu wishes to impress upon Job the truth that God must not be judged to be absent simply because His action is not seen and understood. The god of the heathen is " swallowed up " in an eclipse, but not so the God of the believer. As Cowper says :
          " Ye fearful saints, fresh courage take,
            The clouds ye so much dread
           Are big with mercy, and shall break
           In blessings on your head."
Robert Southey writing on the benefits of affliction expresses a somewhat similar thought thus :
    " If ye would know
    How visitations of calamity
    Affect the pious soul, 'tis shewn ye there !
    Look yonder at that cloud, which, through the sky
    Sailing alone, doth cross in her career
    The rolling moon ! I watched it as it came,
    And deem'd the deep opaque would blot her beams ;
    But, melting like a wreath of snow, it hangs
    In waves of silver round, and clothes
    The orb with richer beauties than her own ;
    Then, passing, leaves her in her light serene."

It is bríght in the úpper-skíes :
A wínd does but páss and it cléars them.

ᵃ Kittel's
text

22 From the Nórth the bríghtness ᵃ cómeth ;
From Gód is the glóry séen ᵃ.

23 Shaddáī we can néver find oút ;
So gréat in pówer and júdgement !
The Abúndant in mércy afflícts not.

24 Thérefore mén should féar Him ;

ᵇ See
Sept.

All wíse-ones of héart pay Him réverence ᵇ.

v. 22.   The *North* is, so to speak, the Olympus of early Hebrew thought.
See Is. xiv. 13 : Ps. xlviii. 2 (3) : but it was also the region from whence the
invader came to Palestine.   See Jer. i. 14 : iv. 6 : vi. 1 &c. : Ezek. i. 4 &c.
Thus Elihu may either mean that the Light breaks forth from the very Home
of God, or, more probably, that it springs from the very source of the trouble.

v. 23.   The metre shews that this verse is wrongly divided in the Masoretic
text.

v. 24ᵇ.   The rendering of the R.V., *He regardeth not any that are wise of*
heart, introduces a discordant note.   The reading which we adopt from the
Septuagint involves little more than a change of vowel points and must be
accepted as harmonising with the thought of Elihu.

INDEX

For EU product safety concerns, contact us at Calle de José Abascal, 56–1°,
28003 Madrid, Spain or eugpsr@cambridge.org.

www.ingramcontent.com/pod-product-compliance
Ingram Content Group UK Ltd.
Pitfield, Milton Keynes, MK11 3LW, UK
UKHW030902150625
459647UK00021B/2659